Kickoff

Workbook Wirtschaft

von
David Christie

Ernst Klett Verlag
Stuttgart · Leipzig

Kickoff – Praxisnahes Englisch für Schule und Beruf

Autor: David Christie, Oxford

Berater: Ilse Halbeck, Hannover; Katrin von Gartzen, Hannover; Melanie Rechmann, Hannover; Martina Ullrich, Düsseldorf; Bernd Deininghaus, Dortmund; Petra Schuster, Bad Dürkheim; Kerstin Streiff, Gießen

Werkübersicht:

Kickoff Schülerbuch	978-3-12-808236-3
Kickoff Lehrerhandbuch mit Audio-CDs (2) und Lehrer-Service-CD	978-3-12-808237-0
Kickoff Workbook – Wirtschaft	978-3-12-808238-7
Kickoff Workbook – Technik	978-3-12-808239-4
Kickoff Workbook – Sozialpädagogik, Hauswirtschaft, Gesundheit	978-3-12-808240-0
Kickoff Lehrer-Workbook für alle Ausrichtungen	978-3-12-808241-7
Kickoff – Vokabeltraining	http://www.klett-kickoff.de
Kickoff – MP3-Audios zum Runterladen	http://www.klett.de/online

1. Auflage 1 5 4 3 2 1 | 2012 2011 2010 2009 2008

Alle Drucke dieser Auflage sind unverändert und können im Unterricht nebeneinander verwendet werden.
Die letzte Zahl bezeichnet das Jahr des Druckes.

Internetadresse: www.klett.de

Abbildungsnachweis Titelseite: Getty Images, Digital Vision; Image Source

Projektleitung: Matthias Rupp
Redaktion: Chris Caridia, Berlin
Gestaltung: Andreas Staiger, B2 : Büro für Gestaltung, Stuttgart
Druck: Media-Print Informationstechnologie GmbH, Paderborn

Printed in Germany.
ISBN 978-3-12-808238-7

9 783128 082387

Unit 1 At college

1 **Ken, Marcie and Ella are students at two different community colleges in the USA. Read what they say and finish the sentences about them below. Use the *simple present*.**

Hi. I'm Ken Kimura and I live in Seattle in the north-west of the United States. I'm a student at the Seattle City College and I'm on a media course. When I finish the course, I want to be a movie cameraman maybe in Hollywood. I go to college five days a week from 9 a.m. to 4 p.m.

Ken

We're Marcie DiMartino and Ella Harris. We live in Washington DC, the US capital and we're students there at the Franklin D. Roosevelt Community College. We're on an IT course. When we finish, we both want to be computer technicians. We're best friends. We go to college together and we often hang out together at the weekend, too.

Marcie and Ella

1 Ken Kamura __lives__ in Seattle.

2 Marcie and Ella ______ in Washington DC.

3 When Ken ______ his course, he ______ to be a cameraman.

4 When Marcie and Ella ______ their course, they ______ to be computer technicians.

5 Ken ______ to college five days a week.

6 Marcie and Ella always ______ to college together – and they often ______ together at the weekend, too.

2 **Make questions about Ken, Marcie and Ella. Use the *simple present*.**

1 **(live)** Where __do__ Marcie and Ella __live__? – In Washington.

2 **(live)** Where ______ Ken ______? – In Seattle.

3 **(want)** What ______ Ken ______ to be after his course? – A cameraman.

4 **(want)** What ______ Marcie and Ella ______ to be? – Computer technicians.

5 **(go)** When ______ Ken ______ to college? – Five days a week.

6 **(do)** What ______ Marcie and Ella often ______ at the weekend? – They often hang out together.

► **capital** Hauptstadt

3 **Read about Özlem then finish the short text about her. Use the *simple present*.**

Name	Özlem Guler
Country	Germany
Town	Dortmund
Course	business administration
After her course	a secretary

Özlem **(1)** doesn't live **(not/live)** in the USA. She **(2)** ________ **(live)** in Dortmund in Germany. She **(3)** ________ **(be)** a student at a Berufsfachschule and she **(4)** ________ **(be)** on a business administration course. After her course, Özlem **(5)** ________ ________ **(not/want)** to be a computer technician and she **(6)** ________________ **(not/want)** to work in Hollywood. She **(7)** ________ **(want)** to be a secretary.

4 **Do the crossword.**

Across
1 *weil:* …
3 *Land:* Germany is a …
6 *Broschüre:* …
7 *dauern:* How long does the lesson …?

Down
2 *Nachmittag:* …
3 *Kurs:* What … are you on?
4 *Kerl:* My friend is a great …
5 *echt:* It would be … cool!
8 *bald:* Hoping to hear from you …

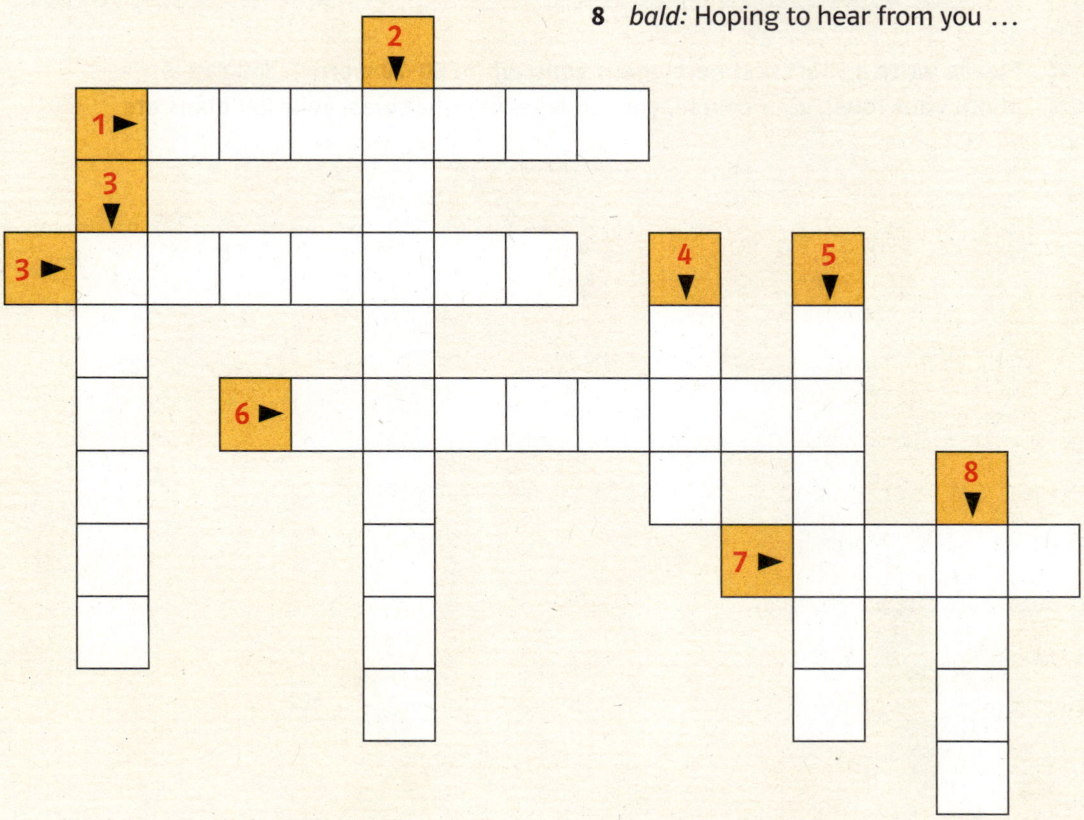

An application form

5 **You want to go on this language course in London. Fill in the application form.**

Hier lerne ich …

- einen Antrag auszufüllen,
- über mich selbst schriftliche Auskunft zu geben.

ENGLISH IN LONDON
APPLICATION FORM

English in London!

Do you want to practise your English? Our course from 15–19 August is for students at vocational colleges around Europe.

For an application form, call Ken Richards on ++ 44 020 714 3000 NOW!

Please write in CAPITAL letters.

Surname ______________________

First name ______________________

Date of birth ______________________

Nationality ______________________

Address (street/number) ______________________

(post code/town) ______________________

(country) ______________________

Telephone number (home) ______________________

(mobile) ______________________

Email address (not capital letters) ______________________

Name and address of college ______________________

____

Please write a short text here about yourself (in 50–70 words). You can write about your town, your course, your college, your hobbies, your job plans etc.

____

____

____

____

____

____

____

____

____

____

____

Unit 2 People and jobs

1 **Match the people in the pictures and the jobs. Write sentences about the people.**

Dennis

Eve

Antonio

Sarah

Liam

Claire

Ed

shop assistant
singer
fitness trainer
secretary
mechanic
hairdresser
nursery assistant
Krankenschwests

1 Dennis is a mechanic.
2 Eve ______
3 Antonio ______
4 Sarah ______
5 Liam ______
6 Claire ______
7 Ed ______

2 **Complete the table with the *-ing* forms of the verbs. Be careful with some verbs (=!). Then finish the sentences. Use the *simple present* and the *present continuous*.**

1 to repair repairing
2 to serve (!) ______
3 to cut (!) ______
4 to write (!) ______
5 to sing ______
6 to play ______
7 to help ______

A Claire often ______ with children.
She ______ with some children now.

B Dennis often ______ cars in his job.
He ______ a car right now.

C Antonio ______ hair every day.
He ______ hair at the moment.

D Sarah ______ lots of emails in her job.
She ______ an email now.

3 **Look back at the people on the last page again. Write sentences about *one* more person like the sentences in exercise 2.**

Liam / Ed / Eve ______________________________

____

____

4 ***Simple present or present continuous?* Finish the text about Martin with the correct forms of the verbs.**

Martin Schuster **(1)** lives **(live)** in Cologne in Germany. He **(2)** ________ **(be)** a barman and he **(3)** ________ **(work)** every day in the bar of a hotel in the city centre. So what does Martin usually do in his job? Well, he **(4)** ________ **(bring)** drinks to the customers in the bar. He often **(5)** ________ **(talk)** to the customers too. And he **(6)** ________ **(wash)** glasses and **(7)** ________ **(clean)** the tables. In the photo, it's 9 o'clock in the evening and Martin **(8)** ________ **(work)** at the moment. Right now, he **(9)** ________ **(bring)** drinks to some customers.

5 **Write *four* sentences about YOU. Write *two* things you often do and *two* things you're doing at the moment.**

I often ______________________________

____

____

____

____

____

6 **Here are some places where people work. Can you write the words?**

1 RAB bar

2 ANSLO ________

3 KARP ________

4 PORKSHOW ________

5 RUNRYES ________

6 ICEFOF ________

7 POSH ________

8 TENFISS BULC ________

► **to clean** putzen

In the office

7 **Match the things 1–14 in the picture and the words in the box. Write the words below.**

office chair | desk | computer screen | mouse | computer keyboard | filing cabinet | telephone | waste bin | letters | poster | calendar | radiator | plant | shelf

1 computer screen
2 ______
3 ______
4 ______
5 ______
6 ______
7 ______
8 ______
9 ______
10 ______
11 ______
12 ______
13 ______
14 ______

8 **Look at the picture again. Find: a pen, a dictionary, a diary, a clock. Where are the things? Write sentences. Use the words and phrases in the box.**

1 The pen is on the desk next to the mouse.
2 The dictionary is ______
3 The diary is ______
4 The clock is ______

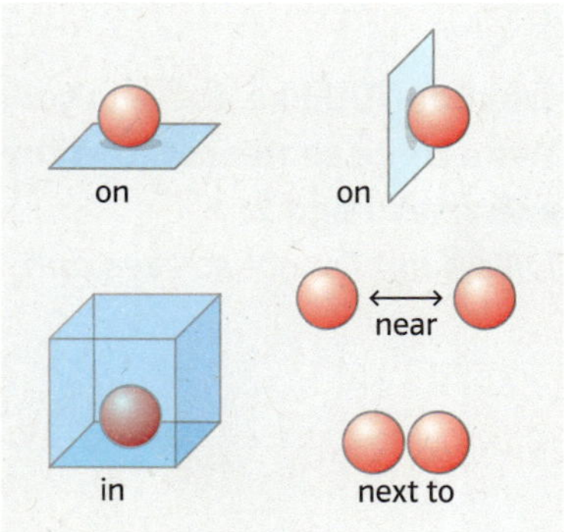

Unit 3 Free time

1 **Match the expressions and the smileys. Write the letters A–D below.**

A I (really) like …

B I love!

C I hate!

D I don't like … (so much) / I'm not keen on …

 ______

 ______

 ______

 ______

2 **WORDSEARCH. Here are 20 words and phrases for free time activities. They are vertical ↓, horizontal → and diagonal ↘. How many can you find? Write the words.**

G	L	P	W	A	T	C	H	I	N	G	T	V	V	Q
O	Y	T	Y	X	K	G	C	A	Z	E	K	Y	O	O
I	M	O	H	O	C	K	E	Y	K	Y	E	J	S	E
N	W	W	G	W	Q	K	F	R	C	G	E	I	D	C
G	J	J	T	A	A	X	O	E	P	L	P	B	W	O
T	S	K	A	T	E	B	O	A	R	D	I	N	G	M
O	R	H	N	G	X	E	T	D	Z	T	N	N	F	P
T	F	B	O	M	U	L	B	I	D	T	G	T	G	U
H	A	C	Q	P	H	Y	A	N	R	K	F	L	R	T
E	D	D	A	J	P	Y	L	G	A	J	I	S	C	E
C	S	B	I	M	U	I	L	Q	M	O	T	P	O	R
I	Z	W	F	U	P	O	N	E	A	G	O	O	O	G
N	S	W	I	M	M	I	N	G	U	G	O	R	K	A
E	B	L	O	G	G	I	N	G	Q	I	T	T	I	M
M	C	H	A	T	T	I	N	G	O	N	L	I	N	E
A	B	Z	C	H	I	L	L	I	N	G	P	P	G	S

20 = excellent! 18–19 = very good 15–17 = good 1–14 = look again

1 ______
2 ______
3 ______
4 ______
5 ______
6 ______
7 ______
8 ______
9 ______
10 ______
11 ______
12 ______
13 ______
14 ______
15 ______
16 ______
17 ______
18 ______
19 ______
20 ______

3 **What do YOU like doing in your free time? What don't you like? Write *three* sentences. Use the words and expressions from exercises 1 and 2:**

I like X but I'm not so keen on Y. I love X and I really like Y, too.

______

______

______

4 **What do you know about London? Finish this article with the *comparative* and *superlative* forms of the adjectives.**

Office workers in the morning in Canary Wharf

LONDON is **(1)** smaller **(small)** than New York (8 million people live in New York and 7.7 million in London) but it is the **(2)** ________ **(big)** city in Europe. It is also one of the **(3)** ________ **(important)** cities in the world for business. One of the **(4)** ________ **(modern)** parts of London is Canary Wharf. Lots of the **(5)** ________ **(large)** companies now have their offices here. Of course, London is also one of the **(6)** ________ **(famous)** cities in the world for tourists. It has five airports, and millions of visitors come to London every year. The **(7)** ________ **(popular)** places are Buckingham Palace (the home of the Queen), the Houses of Parliament, and the London Eye – the **(8)** ________ **(high)** wheel in the world. Travelling in London is easy. There are the famous red buses and six million Londoners travel on them every day. But for tourists in London, the underground is **(9)** ________ **(easy)** than the buses, and often **(10)** ________ **(quick)** too. London has the **(11)** ________ **(old)** underground system in the world: it started in 1863. It is also the **(12)** ________ **(large)** system in Europe. Theatres, cinemas, restaurants, pubs, clubs, museums, parks, shops – London has everything. It is one of the **(13)** ________ **(exciting)** cities in the world.

The London underground. Londoners call it 'the tube'.

► **part** (Stadt) Teil ► **wheel** Rad

A company website

Hier lerne ich …

→ mit dem Internetangebot einer Firma professionell zu arbeiten.

5 **This is the home page of a company in Britain. It sells furniture and other things for offices online. Match the buttons 1–6 and the web pages A–F below. Write in the number of the button.**

Officeweb – *everything for your office!*

- About us 1
- Our products 2
- Shop online 3
- Contact 4
- Careers 5
- News 6

keyword search GO!

Home | About us | Our products | Shop online | Contact | Careers | News

A
Email:
info@officeweb.co.uk
Phone:
(+44) 020 713 9114

[4]

B
Are you interested in a job with Officeweb? For more information email: careers@officeweb.co.uk

[ ]

C
Officeweb is the UK's biggest and best online store for office furniture and equipment. The company started in 1995. Today we have customers around the world.

[ ]

D

office chairs	more …
desks	more …
computers	more …
lamps	more …
calendars	more …
diaries	more …

[ ]

E

OC1479B
£105.00
Add to basket

[ ]

F
Officeweb wins an award for the year's best e-commerce business in the UK.
Read more …

[ ]

6 **Work with a partner. Take it in turns to ask about the website.**

How can I …
- find out about the company? – *You click on the '…' button.*
- get information about the company's products? – *Go to the '…' page.*
- buy products online?
- contact the company direct?
- find out about jobs with the company?
- get news about the company?

7 **Do you buy many things online? What? When? Why? Ask a partner.**

Unit 4 Products then and now

1 **Julie is a modern teenager. Her father lived in the 1970s. What things were the same for her father then and what things were different? Finish the sentences below. Use the *simple past*.**

The same ...

1 Julie likes music. Her father ___liked___ music, too.

2 Julie often goes dancing. Her father often ______ dancing, too.

3 Julie often watches TV. Her father often ______ TV, too.

4 Julie drinks cola. Her father ______ cola, too.

5 Julie often phones her friends. Her father ______ his friends, too.

Different ...

6 Julie listens to music on her MP3 player. Her father ___didn't listen___ to music on an MP3 player. He ___listened___ to records or to his transistor radio.

7 Julie has a colour TV. Her father ______ a colour TV. He ______ a black and white TV.

8 Julie phones her friends on her mobile. Her father ______ his friends on a mobile. He ______ them on an old-fashioned phone.

► **record** Schallplatte ► **old-fashioned** altmodisch

2 **Here are some Quick Facts about pizzas. Make questions and give the answers. Use the *simple past*.**

PIZZA
Quick Facts

First pizzas	People in Greece ate pizzas 2000 years ago.
First modern pizzas	Raffaele Esposito, a baker in Naples, Italy, made the first modern pizza in 1889. It was for the Italian Queen Margherita. He used (red) tomatoes, (white) cheese and (green) basil. The Italian flag is red, white and green.
Pizzas in the USA	An Italian man called Gennaro Lombardi opened the first pizzeria in New York in 1905.
Pizzas in Germany	Another Italian, Nicola di Camillo, opened the first pizzeria in Germany in Wurzburg in 1952.

1 Where ___did___ people ___eat___ **(eat)** the first pizzas?
They ________________ in Greece.

2 When ________ an Italian baker ________ **(make)** the first modern pizza?
He ________________

3 What colours ________ he ________ **(use)?**
____

4 Where ________ Gennaro Lombardi ________ **(open)** the first American pizzeria?
____

5 When ________ Nicola di Camillo ________ **(open)** the first German pizzeria?
____

3 **Finish the time expressions with words on the left. You can use some expressions more than once!**

in
on
last
ago

1 ___last___ week
2 ________ 1955
3 ________ 3 April 1971
4 10 years ________
5 ________ the 1970s
6 ________ year
7 2 weeks ________
8 ________ the 1990s

► **baker** Bäcker ► **Naples** Neapel ► **basil** Basilikum ► **flag** Fahne

Departments in a company

Hier lerne ich …

- → Abteilungen einer Firma zu benennen,
- → über die Arbeit der Abteilungen zu sprechen.

4 **Here are some important departments in a company. Match the English names (A–G) and the German names (1–7).**

A **production** B **sales** C **marketing**

D **distribution** E **finance** F **customer service** G **research and development**

1 Verkauf ____ 2 Kundendienst ____ 3 Produktion ____ 4 Marketing ____

5 Forschung und Entwicklung ____ 6 Vertrieb ____ 7 Finanzen ____

5 **These people are talking about the work of their departments. Which departments do they work in? Write in the English names from exercise 4.**

We transport the company's products.

We advertise the products.

We sell the company's products.

We look after the company's money.

1 ________ 2 ________ 3 ________ 4 ________

We help customers with problems.

We invent new products.

We make the products.

5 ________ 6 ________ 7 ________

6 **Make and answer questions with a partner.**

Which department does Karen work in?

She works in the distribution department.

What does the sales department do?

It sells the company's products.

Unit 5 Do's and don'ts

1 ***Has to*** **or** ***doesn't have to*****? Finish the short texts about Faith and Connie.**

Faith: office worker

Faith lives in Phoenix, Arizona. She's an office worker. She **(1)** has to work every day from 9 a.m. to 5 p.m. At work, she **(2)** ________ wear smart clothes and she **(3)** ________ be polite with her boss and her firm's customers. Sometimes she **(4)** ________ work on Saturdays too. But she **(5)** ________ ________ work on Sundays – that's always her free day.

Connie: student

Connie is a student at a college in Phoenix. She **(6)** ________ work in an office every day from 9 a.m. to 5 p.m. But she **(7)** ________ go to college from Monday to Friday. At college she usually wears jeans – she **(8)** ________ wear smart clothes like Faith. So is Connie's life easy? No! She **(9)** ________ do lots of tests and exams and they're hard!

2 **You're in your town in Germany with a friend from America. You see the signs on the next page. Your friend doesn't speak German. Can you explain the signs in English? Use *must* and *mustn't*.**

A This sign means that you must put (your) rubbish in the rubbish bin.

B ________

____

C ________

D ________

E ________

► **smart** schick ► **polite** höflich ► **exam** Prüfung ► **to explain** erklären

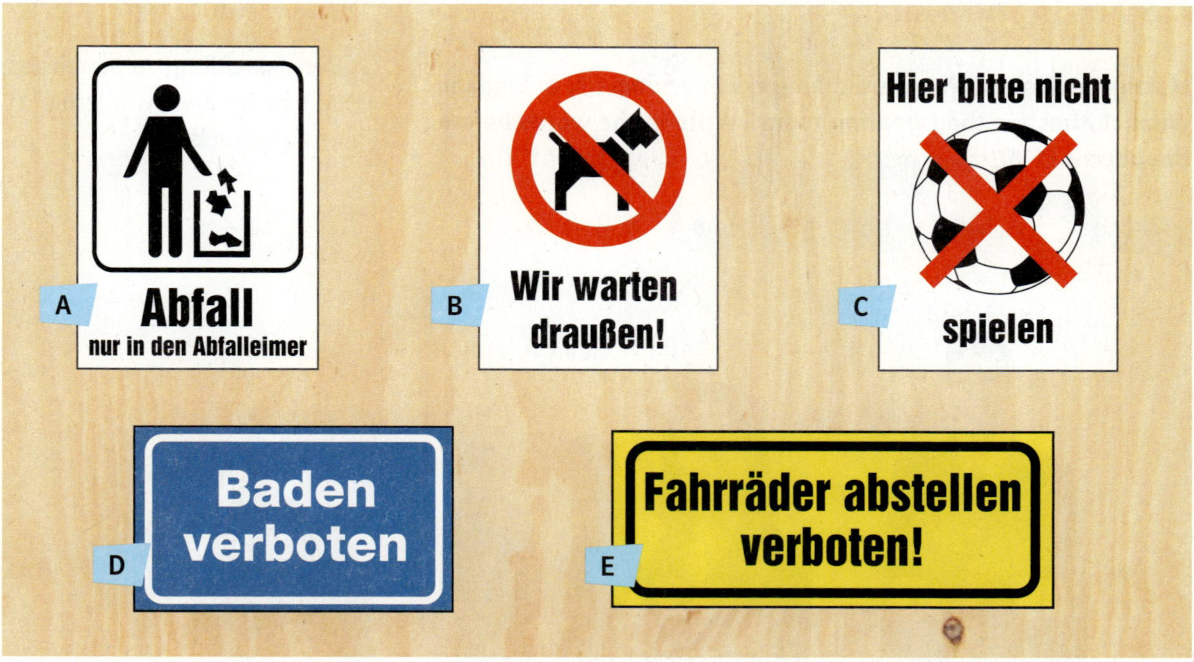

3 **Complete the text with these words and phrases:**

presidents | started | company | old | north | buildings | air | ~~steel workers~~ | hot water | lasted

A dangerous and exciting job!

Timber cutters and **(1)** steel workers have dangerous jobs. They have to work high in the **(2)** ________. But some technicians at the big German **(3)** ________ Kärcher also have a dangerous job. They clean big **(4)** ________ and statues. In 2005, Kärcher technicians cleaned the famous heads of the American **(5)** ________ (Washington, Jefferson, Theodore Roosevelt and Lincoln) on Mount Rushmore in the **(6)** ________ of the USA. They **(7)** ________ on American Independence Day, July 4, and the work **(8)** ________ three weeks. The presidents' heads are 18 metres high and the technicians cleaned them with **(9)** ________. The heads are 65 years **(10)** ________, but they are now very clean again!

Clothes in the office

Hier lerne ich …

- → Berufskleidung zu benennen,
- → zu beschreiben, wie jemand angezogen ist.

4 **Martin, Louise and Peter are managers in a company in England. What clothes are they wearing today? Write in the words below the photos (1–8).**

shirt | shoes | ~~suit~~ | blouse | jacket | tie | trousers | skirt

1 suit
2 ______
3 ______
4 ______
5 ______
6 ______
7 ______
8 ______

5 **Now look at these words. Write sentences about the people.**
Martin is wearing a red tie and a dark suit.
Louise is wearing a striped …

spotted | white | striped | red | grey | dark | reddish-brown

6 **Work with a partner. Partner B: close your book. Partner A: ask questions about Martin, Louise and Peter.**

What's Luise wearing? — She's wearing …

What sort of tie is Martin wearing? — He's wearing a …

Is Louise wearing a white blouse? — No, she's wearing a …

Tips and tricks

Trousers are plural in English: *wearing* ***a*** *tie,* ***a*** *shirt …*
But: *He's wearing* ***trousers***.
His trousers ***are*** *grey.*

Unit 6 Success stories

1 **The five people below work for a firm in Danbury. It's called Danbury Windows Ltd. Write the sentences. Use the *present perfect* and *for* or *since*.**

apprentice carpenter **(1 year)**

office worker **(2006)**

warehouse worker **(2003)**

manager **(4 years)**

receptionist **(a long time!)**

1 Laura is an apprentice carpenter. She has worked in the company for one year.

2 Dan ______________________________

3 Michael ______________________________

4 Carolyn ______________________________

5 Mrs Ellis ______________________________

2 **Here are some more sentences about Laura, Michael and Carolyn. Finish them with the *present perfect* and *for* or *since* again. Be careful! The verbs are irregular.**

1 In her free time, Laura sings in a girl band. She ______________ **(sing)** in the band __________ 2007.

2 Mike's hobby is selling things on eBay. He ______________ **(sell)** things online __________ about six years.

3 Carolyn likes fast cars. She ______________ **(drive)** a Porsche __________ last year.

► **apprentice** Lehrling ► **carpenter** Tischler

3 ***Present perfect* or *simple past*? Finish the article with the correct forms of the verbs.**

FROM GERMANY TO HOLLYWOOD: DJ PATE NUMBER 1

DJ Pate Number 1's real name is Sascha Gerecht. He **(1)** was **(be)** born in a small village near Stuttgart in Germany in 1975. After college in 1996, he **(2)** ______________ **(open)** a dance club in an old warehouse near Stuttgart. It soon **(3)** ______________ **(become)** the most popular club in southern Germany. Then in 2004, he **(4)** ______________ **(perform)** on the 'party' island of Ibiza. Some American guys **(5)** ______________ **(see)** him there and said: "Hey! Come to LA!" Now DJ Pate lives in Los Angeles. He **(6)** ______________ **(live)** there since 2006 and he is one of the most famous and successful DJs in California. He often performs at parties for famous people – like Sylvester Stallone. "I **(7)** ______________ **(want)** to be famous since I was 10 years old," says DJ Pate. "And now I am!"

4 **What are these words from the unit? Do the crossword.**

Across

1 *Lokalzeitung*: … newspaper
4 *Koch/Köchin*: …
6 *lange*: How … have you lived here?
8 *Erfolg*: …
9 *verheiratet*: Jamie Oliver is … to Jools.
10 *veranstalten*: …
11 Another word for 'company': …
14 *arbeitslos*: …
15 *(Geld) verdienen*: … money

Down

2 *namens*: I live in a town … Danbury.
3 *verlassen*: … college
5 *Klempner(in)*: …
7 *Lieblings-*: What's your … band?
12 *(um)ziehen*: He wants to … to London.
13 *Polen*: …

► **warehouse** Lagerhalle ► **real name** echter Name ► **to perform** auftreten

On the phone (1)

Hier lerne ich …

- → jemanden anzurufen,
- → ein Gespräch weiterzuleiten.

5 **Holger Feldmann is a secretary in a firm in Germany. He's calling two people in London this morning. Read his conversations and underline the English for the German phrases.**

1 Bleiben Sie am Apparat, bitte.

2 Könnte ich bitte mit … sprechen?

3 Wer ist am Apparat, bitte?

4 Würden Sie Ihren Namen bitte buchstabieren?

5 Hier ist …

6 Einen Moment, bitte. Ich stelle Sie durch.

Conversation 1

Receptionist	Cordex Engineering Ltd. Good morning.
Holger	Good morning. This is Holger Feldmann from Germany. Could I speak to Mr Rogers, please?
Receptionist	One moment, please, Mr Feldmann. I'll put you through.

Conversation 2

Receptionist	Horizon Software Ltd. Good morning.
Holger	Good morning. Could I speak to Ms Tate, please?
Receptionist	Who's calling, please?
Holger	It's Holger Feldmann from Germany.
Receptionist	Could you spell your name for me?
Holger	Yes, Feldmann. F-E-L-D-M-A-N-N.
Receptionist	Thank you, Mr Feldmann. Hold the line, please. I'll put you through.

6 **Make this conversation with a partner. Partner A: you're the receptionist at Northern Telecom Ltd. in England. Partner B: you're YOU.**

Partner A	Partner B
Melde dich.	
	Melde dich. Du möchtest gern mit Herrn Davis sprechen.
Bitte Partner B ihren/seinen Namen zu buchstabieren.	
	Buchstabiere deinen Namen.
Bedanke dich bei deiner Partnerin/deinem Partner und bitte sie/ihn, am Apparat zu bleiben. Du stellst durch.	

7 **Make another conversation with your partner. Think of names etc. yourselves.**

► Ltd = limited

Unit 7 Looking ahead

1 **It's the end of the year at a college and the students below are planning a party. The tall guy on the left is George. Read what he says about their plans and answer the questions below. Use full sentences.**

Last year they organised the end-of-year party outside. It rained! This year, we aren't going to organise the party outside – we're going to organise it inside, maybe in the local sports centre. Last year they had a disco. This year we're going to look for a live band. Susie (the girl on the right) knows some guys in a band and she's going to contact them. We've got a plan for something totally new this year, too. At midnight, we're going to show a movie.

1 Where did the students organise the end-of-year party last year?

They organised it outside.

2 Where are George and his friends going to organise the party this year?

They ______________________________

3 What music did they have last year?

____

4 What music are George and his friends going to have this year?

____

5 What is Susie going to do?

____

6 They plan something totally new this year. What are they going to do?

____

2 **Correct these sentences.**

George and his friends are going to have a disco this year. Susie is going to be the DJ.

No, they ______________________________

____

____

► **to show** vorführen

3 **George is at a fair in his town. He's with a fortune teller. Read what she says, then look at the sentences A–H below. *Three* sentences are wrong! Find and correct them.**

You'll be married but your wife won't be from England. You'll live with her in another country. You'll have lots of children – ah, they'll all be girls. You won't be rich but you won't be poor. You'll have three jobs in your life. You'll like the first job, but you'll hate the second. You won't have that job very long. The best job will be the third. Something bad will happen when you're 30 and your life will be hard for two or three years. But everything will be OK after that – your life will be long and happy.

A George won't be rich or poor.
B He'll die when he's 30.
C His wife won't be English.
D George's best job will be his second job.
E George will live in another country.
F All George's children will be boys.
G His life will be long and happy.
H George will like his first job.

1 Sentence __B__: George won't __die__
__Something__

2 Sentence ____________________

3 Sentence ____________________

4 **Read about Cherise from the USA. Then finish Gemma's text with British English.**

CHERISE lives with her mom and dad in an apartment in Detroit, Michigan. Her dad is a truck driver. She's a student and she goes to college every day on the subway. On Saturdays she calls her friends on her cell phone and they meet downtown. They look at stores, eat burgers and fries, and go to a movie theater.

GEMMA lives with her **(1)** __mum__ and dad in a **(2)** ________ in Birmingham. Her dad is a **(3)** ________ driver. There isn't an **(4)** ________ in Birmingham so Gemma goes to college by bus. On Saturdays, she calls her friends on her **(5)** ________ and they meet in the **(6)** ________ . They look at **(7)** ________, eat fish and **(8)** ________, and go to a **(9)** ________.

► **fair** Kirmes ► **to happen** geschehen

On the phone (2)

Hier lerne ich ...

→ jemanden anzurufen,
→ Telefonnummern auf Englisch anzugeben.

5 **Holger Feldmann (from Unit 6) is calling a company in Scotland today. Read his conversation and underline the English for the German phrases.**

So gibt man Telefonnummern auf Englisch an:

0 = *oh*
88 = *double* eight
0049 = double oh four nine
511 = five double one
546 = five four six
7139 = seven one three nine
0120 – 658 7155-0 = oh one two oh, six five eight, seven one double five, oh

Receptionist	Good morning. Scottish Electronics Ltd. How can I help you?
Holger	Good morning. This is Holger Feldmann from Germany. Could I speak to Mr MacDonald, please?
Receptionist	I'm sorry, Mr Feldmann. Mr MacDonald isn't here at the moment. Can he call you back this afternoon?
Holger	Oh, yes, thank you.
Receptionist	Can I take your number?
Holger	Yes, it's 0049 for Germany, 511 for Hanover, then 546 7139.
Receptionist	OK. I have all that.
Holger	Great. Thanks. Goodbye.
Receptionist	Bye.

1 Tschüs.
2 Es tut mir leid, ... ist momentan nicht da.
3 Auf Wiederhören.
4 Wie kann ich Ihnen helfen?
5 Kann er/sie Sie zurückrufen?
6 Dürfte ich Ihre Nummer notieren?

6 **Make this conversation with a partner. Partner A: you're the receptionist at Highland Whisky Ltd in Scotland. Partner B: you're YOU.**

Partner A	Partner B
Melde dich.	
	Melde dich. Du möchtest mit Herrn Brown sprechen.
Herr Brown ist leider nicht da. Ob er Partner B morgen zurückrufen darf?	
	In Ordnung.
Bitte Partner B um ihre/seine Telefonnummer.	
	Gib deine Nummer durch.
Alles klar!	
	Verabschiede dich.
Verabschiede dich.	

7 **Make another conversation with your partner. Think of names etc. yourselves.**

Unit 8 A month in New Zealand

1 **Some New Zealand teenagers are at a beach party. Look at what they're saying (A–E) and think of answers.**

A No thanks. It's great but I'm absolutely ____________

B ____________

C ____________

D ____________

E ____________

2 **You're in New Zealand. How can you say the things below in English?**

1 Verzeihung. Könnten Sie mir bitte helfen?

____

2 Wie geht's euch heute morgen?

____

3 (Would you like some more pancakes?) Ja bitte. Sie sind lecker!

____

► **to borrow** ausleihen

3 **Complete this article with the time expressions. Write the letters A–E in the text.**

A ~~at the moment~~ **B** a year ago **C** for **D** in the 1930s **E** next summer **F** right now

Sheep are an important industry in New Zealand. In fact, for every *one* person, there are *12* sheep! Rod Smith is a sheep farmer on the South Island. You can see him in this picture. He's cutting a sheep's wool **(1)** _A_ . Rod's grandparents came to New Zealand from England **(2)** _____ . They bought a farm. Rod and his wife still live on the farm today, so the Smith family have lived there **(3)** _____ over 60 years. Martine Smith is Rod's daughter. You can see her in the photo above. She's driving her dad's car **(4)** _____ . Martine is a college student. She started her course **(5)** _____ . Martine is on an agriculture course. When she finishes the course **(6)** _____ , she's going to work on the farm too. Martine will be the fourth generation of the Smith family on the farm.

4 **Translate the text in exercise 3 into German. Write on a separate piece of paper.**

5 **Many job names in English end in *-er* like in German. But not all! Finish the words.**

1	Bauer	farm _er_	**5**	Büroarbeiter	office work _____
2	Friseur	hairdress _____	**6**	Maurer	bricklay _____
3	Mechaniker	mechan _____	**7**	Schauspieler	act _____
4	Elektriker	electric _____	**8**	Regisseur	film direct _____

► **wool** Wolle ► **farm** Bauernhof ► **agriculture** Landwirtschaft

At the reception desk

Hier lerne ich …

→ eine/n Besucher/in im Betrieb korrekt zu empfangen.

6 **Judith Meyer is a receptionist in a company in Germany. She's talking to a visitor to the company. Read her conversation with a partner.**

Judith Guten Tag.
Man Er. Do you speak English?
Judith Yes of course. Good morning. Can I help you?
Man Oh, thanks. Good morning. I have an appointment with Mr Kessler at 10.30.
Judith Can I take your name, please?
Man Hammersmith. That's H-A-M-M-E-R-S-M-I-T-H.
Judith Ah yes Mr Hammersmith. Could you fill in the visitors' book for me? The date, your name, your time of arrival, and your signature, please.
Man OK. Here you are.
Judith Thank you. And here's your visitor's badge. Please wear it at all times.
Man Thank you.
Judith Please take a seat over there. Would you like a tea or a coffee while you're waiting?
Man No thanks.
Judith Fine. Mr Kessler will be here soon.

7 **Work with a partner. Partner A: you are the receptionist. Partner B: you are a visitor. Change the names in the dialogue in exercise 6 and make a new conversation. Write in the visitors' book below and make a name badge, too. Can you do make the dialogue with your books closed?**

VISITOR
Mr N. Hammersmith

Datum (date)	Name (name)	Ankunft (time in)	Abfahrt (time out)	Unterschrift (signature)
12th June	N. Hammersmith	10:25		N. Hammersmith

Unit 9 Travel

1 **Look at the airport photos A–D. What can you see? What's happening? What are the people doing? Write sentences with the verbs in the box.**

buy
choose
drink
eat
shop
sit
~~take off~~
talk
use
work

1 The plane in picture A is taking off.
2 The people in picture B ____________ in a café at the airport.
3 They ____________
4 The two business guys in picture C ____________
5 They ____________
6 The two girls in picture D ____________
7 They ____________

2 **Write these sentences again. Put in *often, always, usually,* or *sometimes*. (You can choose.)**

1 The two business guys work at the airport.
2 They use a laptop.
3 Claudia (one of the girls) doesn't buy clothes at the airport. (But today they're cheap.)

1 The two business guys
2 ____________
3 ____________

3 **Travel crossword. First, finish the definitions with *who, which* or *where*, then write the words into the crossword. All the words are about travel.**

Down

1 The form which you fill in when you arrive at a hotel is a … form.

2 A person ________ travels by plane, train etc. is a …

3 The place ________ people check your clothes and baggage at an airport is the … check.

5 The thing ________ opens the door of your hotel room.

6 The things ________ you carry when you travel.

8 The person ________ checks in people at an airport is a check-in …

10 The place ________ you go for your plane.

11 Someone ________ checks your bags when you arrive at an aiport.

14 Someone ________ isn't a child and is over 18 is an …

Across

1 A man or woman ________ works at the reception desk in a hotel is a …

4 A small book ________ gives you information (e.g. about a hotel).

7 A man ________ works in business.

9 A room ________ is for one person.

12 The document ________ you get when you check in at an airport and ________ gives you your gate number is a … card.

13 Something ________ you need when you travel to another country.

15 The place ________ you check in at an airport is the check-in … and at a hotel it's the reception …

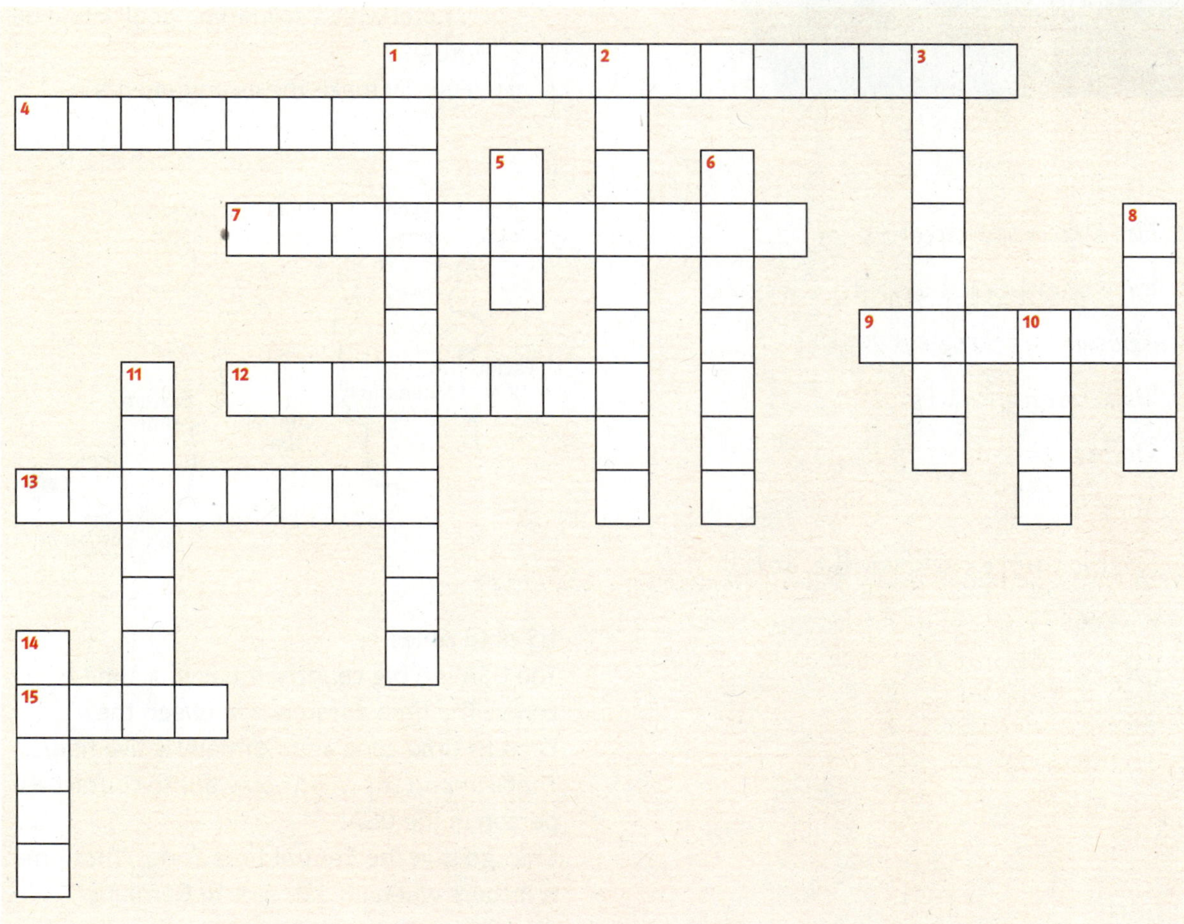

Booking a hotel room

Hier lerne ich …

→ ein Hotelzimmer zu buchen,
→ eine Faxbestätigung zu schreiben.

4 **Leonie Koch is a secretary in an American company in Germany. Her boss is Joe Rosenberg. Next week, Mr Rosenberg will be in the States. He's talking to Leonie about his trip. Read their conversation, then complete Leonie's notes below.**

Leonie When will you be in Chicago, Mr Rosenberg?
Joe On Wednesday and Thursday next week.
Leonie That's October 17 and 18.
Joe Right. My first meeting on Wednesday is at 9.30, so I'll need a hotel for the night before, Tuesday night.
Leonie And when will you leave Chicago?
Joe My last meeting there finishes at midday on Thursday. Then I'll fly to Seattle.
Leonie So you don't want to stay overnight on Thursday?
Joe No, I'll take a plane on Thursday afternoon.
Leonie And about the hotel. You just want a single room, right? Anything else special?
Joe Yes, a single room. The hotel should be near the city centre, if possible. Oh, and a hotel with a swimming pool would be great.
Leonie Fine. I'll make the arrangements.

Hotel arrangements for
Mr Rosenberg's trip to Chicago:
Room: single room
Number of nights: ____________
Dates: ____________

Special notes about the hotel:
Where? ____________
Other: ____________

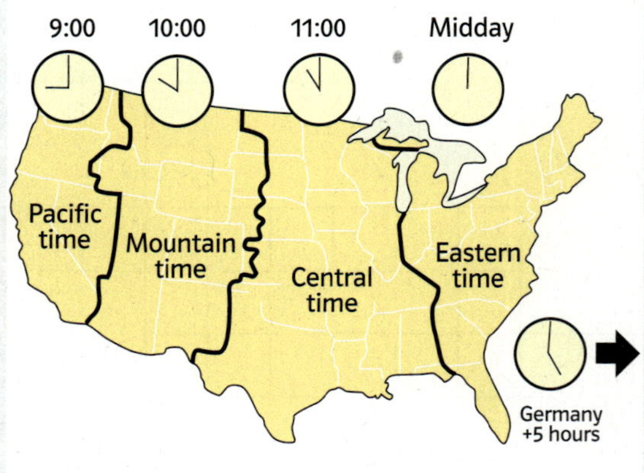

US time zones
The USA is a big country. It has four time zones. The time difference between the Eastern Time Zone and Germany is five hours. That's important when you want to contact a person in the USA!
Chicago is in the Central Time Zone. What time is it there when it's 9.00 a.m. in Germany?

5 **Finding a hotel. Leonie looked on the Internet for hotels for Mr Rosenberg. Here are two. Which one is better? Why? Write one or two sentences below.**

O'Hare Inn, Chicago ★★★★

Rooms	325
Location	O'Hare International Airport, Chicago. Only 2 minutes from the airport terminal. Ideal for business travelers.
Facilities	Restaurant, bar, fitness center, parking, Internet access, 4 conference centers

Belmont Hotel, Chicago ★★★★

Rooms	214 all smoke free
Location	Downtown Chicago. One block from the John Hancock Center, Water Tower and Magnificent Mile shopping
Facilities	Restaurant, bar, sauna, swimming pool, fitness center, parking, roof garden, Internet access

I think the best hotel is ____________________ because ____________________

____

6 **Next Leonie phones the hotel to make a booking. Read the conversation with a partner. Then change the dates, days, rooms, names etc. and make a new conversation yourselves.**

Receptionist *Belmont, Chicago.* Anita speaking. How may I help you this morning?
Leonie Good morning. I'd like to book a room, please.
Receptionist Certainly. Could you give me the dates, please?
Leonie It's for *two nights from Tuesday October 16 to Thursday October 18.*
Receptionist And is that a single or a double room?
Leonie A *single room.*
Receptionist Smoking or non-smoking?
Leonie *Non-smoking.*
Receptionist Yes, that looks fine. Can I take your name?
Leonie The room is for *Mr Joe Rosenberg, that's R-O-S-E-N-B-E-R-G, from Star Communications in Germany.*
Receptionist Will *Mr Rosenberg* pay for the room personally?
Leonie *No, the company will pay.*
Receptionist Thank you. That's all booked. Could you send me a fax to confirm the booking?
Leonie Sure, I'll do that straight away.
Receptionist Thank you. And thank you for choosing the *Belmont Hotel.*
Leonie Thank you. Goodbye.
Receptionist Bye now.

7 **Leonie sends a fax to the hotel after her conversation. Find the English for these words and phrases.**

1 Fax-Nummer ____________________

2 Betreff ____________________

3 Hiermit bestätige ich ____________________

4 Bitte beachten Sie ____________________

5 in voller Höhe ____________________

FAX

Star Communications GmbH & Co
121 Hofstraße
06886 Wittenberg
Germany
Fax: +49-3491-6200

To:	Reservations, Belmont Hotel, Chicago, IL
Fax Number:	001-773-488-3030
Date:	200..-September-23
Subject:	Confirmation of telephone reservation
From:	Leonie Koch, Star Communications GmbH & Co, Germany

This is to confirm the room reservation made today by telephone for Mr J. Rosenberg from our company:

Dates: Two nights, October 16 and 17
Room: Single room

Please note that Star Communications will pay Mr Rosenberg's bill directly and in full.

Leonie Koch

Faxen
In der heutigen elektronischen Welt werden Faxen weniger benutzt als E-Mails. Dennoch werden sie weiterhin verwendet, um Originaldokumente zu senden oder – wie hier – ein Dokument mit Unterschrift zu schicken.

So läuft's besser
Hier und in den folgenden Units lernst du viel über Korrespondenz. Dabei gibt es eine Reihe wichtige Redewendungen, die du dir merken solltest. Beginne jetzt schon, Lernlisten anzulegen und versuche diese regelmäßig durchzulesen.

8 **Now YOU. Look back to your conversation with a partner in exercise 6. Write a fax to confirm your booking. (You can also invent new details, dates, addresses etc.)**

Unit 10 A visit to a company

1 **Finish the sentences. The words on the left are *adjectives*. The words on the right are *adverbs*.**

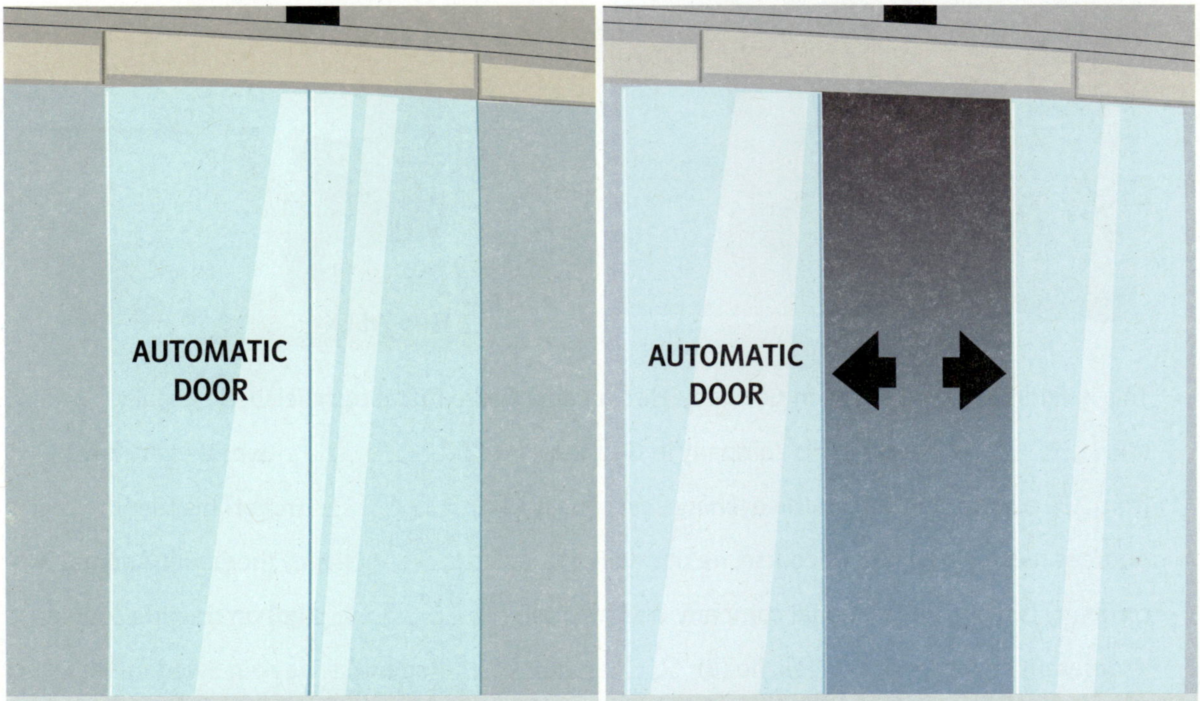

This is an **automatic** door. **(adjective)** It opens **automatically**. **(adverb)**

1 Planes are quick.	They travel ____________.
2 Boats are ____________.	They travel slowly.
3 You must be careful!	Do that ____________!
4 German people are usually ____________.	They usually arrive punctually.
5 Is this an ____________ diagram?	Yes, I drew it exactly.
6 This exercise is easy.	I can do it ____________.
7 William is a bad driver.	He drives very ____________.
8 But Harry is a good driver.	He drives very ____________.

2 **Now finish these sentences with an *adjective* or an *adverb*. Use words from exercise 1. (There is sometimes more than one answer).**

1 Is it an ____________ process?

– Yes, computers and robots do everything in the factory.

2 Don't be late. We must arrive at the railway station ____________.

3 Hey, great Sam! You're an expert! You did that really ____________!

4 That machine is dangerous. You must use it ____________.

5 Could you send us a ____________ answer to our email, please? We need the information today.

3 **Finish the sentences with the verbs. Use the *simple present* or the *present continuous*.**

This is Andreas from Leipzig in Germany. He's an apprentice metal technician. He usually **(1)** works **(work)** in his company in Germany. He **(2)** ____________ **(work)** every day from 7.30 a.m. to 3.00 p.m. In the evenings, he usually **(3)** ____________ **(meet)** his friends. Andreas has his own flat. Of course, he normally **(4)** ____________ **(sleep)** there. But Andreas's company is a big, international company, and he often **(5)** ____________ **(go)** on training courses in different countries. This week, he **(6)** ____________ **(spend)** a week in Sweden. He **(7)** ____________ **(not/work)** in his company and he **(8)** ____________ **(not/sleep)** in his flat. He **(9)** ____________ **(learn)** about new technology and he **(10)** ____________ **(sleep)** at the training centre.

4 **How does a company produce its products? First, put the phrases on the left in the correct order 1–6, then write a short text. Use *first, then, next, after that, finally.***

- [ ] to check products (quality control technicians)
- [ ] to store raw materials in factory
- [ ] to dispatch products from warehouse
- [1] to buy raw materials (office)
- [ ] to store products in warehouse
- [ ] to make products in production area

First, people in the company's office buy the raw materials. Then, the company ____________

____

____

____

____

____

____

____

____

► **metal technican** Metalltechniker ► **training centre** Weiterbildungszentrum

An enquiry

Hier lerne ich …

- → den Aufbau eines englischen Geschäftsbriefs,
- → eine einfache Anfrage zu schreiben.

5 **Read the text below and answer the questions.**

Business partners

One of the most important things in business is contact between companies. Companies sell products (or services), other companies buy them. For example, a company makes and sells pizzas. It needs boxes for the pizzas, so it finds a company which makes boxes. The two companies are now business partners.

So how do companies find a business partner? One possibility is from an advertisement in a trade journal. A trade journal is a magazine for an industry. There are hundreds of these journals – for plastics, manufacturing, communications, food and many other industries. Many trade journals are now also online. A second possibility is a trade fair. Companies show their products here and visitors from around the world can see them. Germany is famous for its trade fairs and there are fairs in many German cities. A third possibility is that a company finds out about a new business partner from an old business partner. For example, one day someone from the pizza company is talking to someone from the box company and says: "Now we have our pizzas and we have your boxes, but we need some lorries so that we can deliver our pizzas." "We bought some lorries last year from Company X," says the other person. "They're good." Tips like this are very helpful!

Business tips from one of your business partners are very helpful.

1 What is a 'business partner'? Give an example.

____

____

2 Where can you often find advertisements for products and services?

____

3 What happens at trade fairs? Is there one in your town or city?

____

____

4 'Talking in business is very important'. How can this be helpful? Give an example.

____

____

6 Read this business letter.

1 What's the writer's name? When (on what date) did she write the letter? To what company and in what country?

____

2 What company does the writer work for? What's her job in the company?

____

3 The writer doesn't know the name of the person he or she is writing to. How can you see this from the letter?

____

4 What is the letter about (the 'subject' of the letter)?

____

letterhead (Briefkopf): the address of the writer's company

GOLTZPROJEKTBAU GmbH
Naumannstraße 18, 60318 Frankfurt am Main
Tel. +49 (69) 335519 E-Mail: Info@Goltz.de

inside address (Empfängeranschrift)

date

Rolac PLC
101–108 Commerce Road
MILTON KEYNES
GB-MK8 4DW

15 September 20..

salutation (Anrede): All letters begin with *Dear …* When you know the person's name, you write *Dear Mr/ Ms …* When you don't know the person, you write *Dear Sir or Madam*.

subject (Betreffzeile): This goes **after** the *Dear …*

Dear Sir or Madam,

Request for sales catalogue and price lists

Letters in English begin with a CAPITAL letter!

We were interested in your paints at the recent trade fair in Frankfurt am Main.

We are a German construction company which builds homes and offices around Europe.

Could you please send us your current sales catalogue and price lists. We would also be grateful for information about your delivery times and trade discounts which you offer.

We look forward to hearing from you soon.

Yours faithfully,

close (Grussformel): Letters which begin *Dear (name)* end with *Yours sincerely*. Letters which begin *Dear Sir or Madam* end *Yours faithfully*.

M. Hochstedt

Marianne Hochstedt
PURCHASING MANAGER

signature (Unterschrift): name and the writer's job below

7 **Look at the letter again and find the English for these words and phrases.**

1 Bitte um/Anforderung ______________________

2 (Verkaufs)katalog und Preislisten ______________________

3 kürzlich stattgefunden ______________________

4 Wir sind ein deutsches Unternehmen, das … ______________________

5 Schicken Sie uns bitte … ______________________

6 aktuell ______________________

7 Wir wären auch für … dankbar. ______________________

8 Lieferzeiten und Handelsrabatte ______________________

9 Wir freuen uns, bald von Ihnen zu hören. ______________________

8 **Now YOU. Write the letter below. Use the letter layout on the last page. Think of a name and address for your German company. There are more words and expressions below to help you.**

You are the purchasing manager of a company in Germany which makes printers *(Drucker)* for PCs and home offices. You need a business partner who can make cables *(Kabeln)* for your printers. You find out about a company in Britain called ADC Cables Ltd. (At a trade fair? From an advertisement in a trade journal?) The company's address is: 27 Mill Road, Birmingham BM6 7UT. Write to the company and ask for their catalogue and price lists. You would also like information about delivery times and trade discounts.

So läuft's besser

Hefte alle Briefe, die du hier und später schreibst in einem Dossier ab. Du kannst sie dann immer nachschlagen.

Enquiry letters			
We were interested in	your (products) at the recent trade fair in … your advertisement in this month's *Electrical World* (trade journal).		
We are a	German company which …		
Could you please send us	your current sales catalogue. price lists. samples of your products.		
We would also	be grateful for like	information about details of	delivery times. trade discounts.
Thank you	in advance for your help.		
We look forward to	hearing from you soon/shortly.		

Unit 11 Future technology

1 **Read this short story. Finish the sentences in the story with the verbs. Use the *simple present* or the *will* future.**

LAD AND HIS FRIEND MIKKO were at Lad's house. It was a Saturday afternoon in the year 2074. "Look here," said Lad. "On the information wall. There's an ad for a time vacation."

"Those time vacations are *really* expensive," said Mikko. "If we **(1)** ___book___ **(book)** this vacation today, it **(2)** ___'ll be___ **(be)** half price," said Lad. " Come on, let's go for it!"

Two weeks later, Lad and Mikko were at the offices of *Time Vacations PLC*. There were 15 people in their group, and a young woman called Jodie. "Listen, please," said Jodie. "We'll leave for our time holiday in ten minutes. You'll visit the earth 200 million years ago – at the time of the dinosaurs. But first, there's one very, very important thing. You mustn't touch anything on your holiday." "Why?" asked Lad. "If you **(3)** __________ **(touch)** anything," answered Jodie, "you **(4)** __________ **(change)** the future. And if you **(5)** __________ the future, we **(6)** __________ **(come back)** to a very different world after our holiday. OK. Is everybody ready? Let's go!"

Lad, Mikko and the other time travellers went into the time room with Jodie. There was a bright light, then they were on earth 200 million years ago. "Wow!" said Mikko. "Look at those dinosaurs. They're enormous! If they **(7)** __________ **(come)** near us, I **(8)** __________ **(run)**!" "No," said Jodie. "We **(9)** __________ **(go)** home if there **(10)** __________ **(be)** a problem. Don't run. You *must* stay here on the path. If you **(11)** __________ **(leave)** the path, you **(12)** __________ **(touch)** something, perhaps."

Two hours later, the time vacation was almost over. "Just one more thing," said Jodie. "If you **(13)** __________ **(look)** over there, you **(14)** __________ **(see)** …" But she didn't

► **bright light** helles Licht ► **path** Weg

finish the sentence. Suddenly, a pterodactyl – an enormous, flying dinosaur – flew towards them. Lad fell to the ground. And he put his hand into the grass near the path. He looked at his hand. In it, there was a beautiful butterfly. Lad put the butterfly in his pocket. "I think we **(15)** ________________ **(go)** home now if you **(16)** __________ **(be)** all ready," said Jodie. She took a small machine from her pocket, there was the bright light again, and then they were back on earth in the year 2074.

Lad and Mikko were in the street. "I brought something from the vacation," said Lad. He showed Mikko the butterfly. "You're crazy!" said Mikko. "Jodie said …" "I know," answered Lad. "You **(17)** ______________________ **(change)** the future if you **(18)** ____________ **(touch)** anything. But it's only a butterfly. And the world looks, well, normal. So there isn't a problem."

Just then, two dogs walked past. "Good morning," said one of the dogs. Lad and Mikko looked at the dog. "But you're a dog," said Lad. You can't talk." "Of course we can talk," said the dog. "All dogs can talk. In fact, we're police dogs. And if you **(19)** __________ **(be)** rude again, we **(20)** ______________________ **(arrest)** you!"

2 **Complete the word puzzle on climate change. (Tip: all the words are in the text on page 111 of your Student's Book.)**

1 SPSs are solar power …
2 We can get energy from the sun, the sea, and the …
3 SPSs will send the sun's energy to earth as …
4 Coal, oil and gas are … fuels.
5 Global … is when the earth's atmosphere becomes warmer.
6 Energy from the sun is … energy.
7 A special sort of train with one rail.
8 The thing which is changing today.
9 ‚Schaden'
10 The opposite of 'dirty'.
11 If we don't change our lives, the future will be a …

1					S	A	T	**E**	L	L	I	T	E	S
2								**N**						
3								**V**						
4								**I**						
5								**R**						
6								**O**						
7								**N**						
8								**M**						
9								**E**						
10								**N**						
11								**T**						

► **butterfly** Schmetterling ► **to arrest** verhaften

An offer

3 **Read the text below and find the English words 1–9 for these German words.**

[2] Angebot	[ ] Preis	[ ] Fracht
[ ] Hafen	[ ] Produkt(e)	[ ] Versicherung
[ ] Lieferzeiten	[ ] Rabatt	[ ] Zahlungsbedingungen

We'd like to buy your food!

One of Germany's important exports is food – another, of course, is wine. A shop in London called the German Food Centre sells German food and wine. A month ago, Ann Culver from the German Food Centre saw some German food **(1)** *products* at a trade fair. They were from a German exporter called Feine Küche GmbH. Ms Culver liked the products and took one of the firm's brochures. On 12 October, she wrote a letter to Feine Küche GmbH. In the letter, she asked for a **(2)** *quotation* for some products. Why did she need a quotation before she bought the products?

When you or I go into a shop to buy a pair of trainers, it's very easy. The trainers cost x euros. We pay our money and we leave. In business, things are more complicated – especially in international trade. First, the **(3)** *price* is not so fixed. Products are usually cheaper if you buy lots of them. If a shop buys 500 pairs of trainers, the price will be lower than for us when we buy one pair. This is called a **(4)** *discount*. Even more important is the question: What does the price include? The basic price of a product is called the 'ex-works' *(ab Werk)* price. But many prices also include **(5)** *transport* and **(6)** *insurance* to the the buyer's shop, or country, or a **(7)** *port* in the country. A typical price is a 'Delivered Ex Quay' price or DEQ *(geliefert ab Kai)*. This means that it includes the cost of transport (and usually insurance) to a port in the buyer's country.

Ms Culver will also want to know two more important facts. First, when will Feine Küche GmbH deliver her products? In other words, she will want to know about **(8)** *delivery times*. Finally, she will want to know when she must pay. In the shop we pay immediately for our trainers. In business people often pay later. The date the buyer must pay is called the **(9)** *terms of payment* and a typical example is 'payment in full within 30 days'.

For all these reasons, Ms Culver needs an offer from Feine Küche GmbH before she buys.

4 **True or false? Tick (√) the correct box.**

		true	false
1	Ann Culver works in a shop in London.	☐	☐
2	She saw some German food products in a magazine.	☐	☐
3	If you get a discount, the price of a product will be lower.	☐	☐
4	A DEQ price is the price plus transport (and often insurance) to the buyer's shop.	☐	☐
5	The terms of payment tell you when a company will deliver your products.	☐	☐

5 **Here is Ms Culver's letter to Feine Küche GmbH. Read the letter and answer the questions below.**

THE GERMAN FOOD CENTRE
18 Covent Garden Street, London W1A 2BW

Feine Küche GmbH
Heilsbrunnstraße 18
53112 Bonn
Germany

12 October 20. .

Dear Sir or Madam,

Request for a quotation

We were impressed by the products on display on your stand at the World Food Exhibition in London last week.

Would you please send us a quotation DEQ Harwich for the following:

50 cases German Sausage Catalogue Number W133-H
40 cases Blackforest Ham Catalogue Number S8871
10 cases German Chocolate Biscuits Catalogue Number K987-E23
50 cases German Riesling Wine Catalogue Number W4-444-5R

We would also be grateful for details of discounts which you can offer us, your delivery times and your terms of payment.

We look forward to hearing from you soon.

Yours faithfully,

A Culver

Ms A Culver
Buyer

Finish the sentences with information from the letter.

1 The name of the trade fair where Ann Culver saw the German company's products was the

______________________________.

2 The port where the German company should send the products is ____________________.

3 Ms Culver gives the products she wants and their ____________________ Number.

4 She also wants to know about discounts and the German company's __________ __________

______________________________.

5 At the end of the letter, Ann writes her job in the British company: she says that she is a

______________________________.

6 **Here is the reply to Ann Culver. Can you fill in the missing words?**

FEINE KÜCHE GmbH Heilsbrunnstraße 18 | 53112 Bonn | Germany

The German Food Centre

(1) ______________________________

LONDON W1A 2BW

18 October 20..

Dear Ms (2) ____________,

Your request for a quotation of (3) ______ October 20..

Thank your for your request for a (4) ______________ and for your interest in our products. We are pleased to send you the following offer:

Quantity	Description	Price (€)	Total (€)
50	Cases German sausage	40.00	2,000.00
40	Cases ham	60.00	2,400.00
10	Cases chocolate biscuits	30.00	300.00
50	Cases wine	100.00	5,000.00
GRAND TOTAL			9,700.00

These prices are (5) __________ Harwich and include a trade discount of 5%.
You can normally expect to receive the goods around one week after we receive your order.

Our (6) ____________ payment are payment in full within 30 days.

I look forward to receiving your order in the near future. Please do not hesitate to contact me if you have any further questions.

Yours (7) ____________,

Roland Maurer

Roland Maurer
Export Manager

7 **Now YOU. Work with a partner. Partner A and Partner B each write to your partner's company for a quotation. Think of a company name, products etc. yourselves. Then exchange letters and write a reply. Use the phrases below.**

Asking for a quotation

Thank you for your sales catalogue.
We were impressed by your products at the trade fair in … last …
Could you please send us a quotation DEQ *(port)* for the following:
We would also be grateful for / We would also like details of / information about …
We look forward to hearing from you / receiving your quotation soon.

Sending a quotation (an offer)

Thank you for your request for a quotation of … *(date)*.
We are pleased to send you / have pleasure in sending you the following offer:
These prices are EXW/DEQ *(port)*.
They include a (trade) discount of …%.
We normally deliver / You can normally expect to receive goods from us … days after we receive your order.
Our terms of payment are payment in full within 30 days / payment in advance.
We look forward to receiving your order soon/shortly.
Please do not hesitate to contact me if you have any further questions / if I can help you further.

Unit 12 Job hunting

1 **Read about these three jobs from around the world.**

OTHER COUNTRIES, OTHER JOBS

1

Country: Canada
Job: mountain rescue worker
In western Canada, there are some high mountains. They're called the Rocky Mountains (or 'the Rockies'). Mountain rescue workers rescue people in the mountains. The job can be hard and dangerous.

2

Country: USA
Job: deli assistant
New York is famous for its delis (delicatessens) where you can buy deli sandwiches and bagels. Deli assistants make sandwiches and serve customers. There are always lots of customers and the assistants work very quickly!

3

Country: Australia
Job: road train driver
Road trains are monster lorries 50 metres long. They have over 60 wheels and they travel at 100 kph. Road train drivers travel all over Australia. They're often on the road for days and they sleep at night in their lorries. The job can be lonely!

2 **Finish the sentences about the jobs. All the sentences are *if*-sentences type 2.**

1 If you had the job in text 1, you would be in ______________ *(country?)*.

2 If you __________ **(have)** the job in text 2, you ______________ **(be)** in New York.

3 You ______________ **(be)** in ______________ *(country?)* if you _______ **(have)** the job in text 3.

4 If you were a mountain rescue worker, you __________________________ *(do what?)*.

5 You __________________ **(make)** sandwiches if you __________ **(be)** a deli assistant.

6 If you __________ **(be)** a road train driver, you ____
__________ *(do what?)*.

► **mountain rescue** Bergwacht ► **to rescue** retten ► **wheel** Rad ► **lonely** einsam

3 **Look back at 'Other countries, other jobs' again on the last page. Answer these questions in full sentences. Use *if-sentences type 2* again.**

1 What mountains would you work in if you were a mountain rescue worker in Canada?
If I was a mountain rescue worker in Canada, I would work in the ______

2 How would you work if you worked in a deli in New York? *(quickly? slowly?)*
If ______

3 Where would you sleep at night if you drove a road train in Australia?
If ______

4 **Complete the job ads with the words and phrases in the box.**

WANTED

MECHANIC (1) to work in our busy car repair workshop. Applicants must be **(2)** ______.
For further **(3)** ______, please **(4)** ______ Martin Reynolds on (0212) 743-744.

part time | contact | careers@techno.com | ~~to work~~ | looking for | Hours | experience | skills | information | fully qualified

We are (5) ______ a

SECRETARY

to work **(6)** ______ in our office. **(7)** ______:
Mon–Thurs. 9 a.m. – 1 p.m.
Applicants must have good computer **(8)** ______ and have **(9)** ______ in office work.
Interested? Please email us at:
(10) ______

5 **Your German friend wants to have a list of the most important 'job hunting' expressions in English and German. Choose expressions from the unit. Copy the table below and continue the list on another piece of paper.**

job hunting – die Arbeitssuche

English	German
job ad(vertisement)	Stellenanzeige
to apply for	sich um ... bewerben

An order

6 Read about Heiko Versand and look at the letter below.

Heiko Versand is a German company which sells goods on the Internet. Ten days ago, it asked a company in Ireland for a quotation for some hockey equipment. Heiko liked the quotation and today the company wants to order some products. You can see the letter below.

HEIKO VERSAND AG
Prinzenstraße 101, 99084 Erfurt, Germany

O'Malley Sports Ltd
8 O'Connell Street
Dublin, 8
Republic of Ireland

18 May 20..

Dear Mr Connor,

Trial Order

Thank you for your offer of 8 May. We would like to place a trial order with you for the following items.

Item	Catalogue number	Quantity	Price
Hockey sticks	HS203	100	€3000
Hockey balls	HB1-B	500	€4000
Helmets	PH005	20	€450
Hockey shoes	D49-TTR	500	€15000

We note that all prices are DEQ Hamburg and include a trade discount of 10%. Payment will be made immediately on receipt of the consignment.

We look forward to receiving the consignment soon.

Yours sincerely,
Bastian Meyer
Bastian Meyer

7 Fill in the missing information.

A German company, Heiko Versand, wants to buy some **(1)** hockey equipment from an Irish company called **(2)** ____________ Ltd. Heiko got a quotation from the Irish company on **(3)** ____________ *(date)* and wrote back with their order on **(4)** ____________. The prices of the items are all DEQ **(5)** ____________ and Heiko will pay for the items immediately **(6)** ____________

8 **O'Malley Sports Ltd received Heiko Versand's order on 20 May. Mr Connor wrote this letter.**

O'MALLEY SPORTS LTD
8 O'Connell Street • Dublin, 8 • Republic of Ireland

Heiko Versand AG
Prinzenstraße 101
99084 Erfurt
Germany

20 May 20..

Dear Mr Meyer,

Your order of 18 May 20..

Thank you for your order of 18 May which we received today. You will receive the goods in 14 days.

We are sure that you will be very satisfied with our products and we look forward to receiving further orders in the future.

Yours sincerely,

Robert Connor

Robert Connor
Export Manager

9 **Now YOU. Work with a partner. Write a letter to your partner's firm to order some products. Then exchange letters and write a reply to the order. Use the phrases below.**

Placing an order

- Thank you for your offer/quotation of ... (date).
- We would like to order / We would like to place an order / a trial order for the following items/products ...
- We note that these prices are ... (DEQ Hamburg).
- We understand that these prices include a discount of ...%.
- Payment will be made immediately on receipt of the goods/the consignment/the products.
- We look forward to receiving the consignment/goods/products soon/shortly.

Acknowledging an order

- Thank you / Many thanks for your order of ... (date) for our products.
- You will receive the consignment in ... days / on ... (date) / within ... weeks.
- We are sure that / We know that you will be satisfied/pleased with our products.
- We look forward to receiving further orders in the future.
- If there are any problems/questions, please contact me/us immediately.

10 **Read the text and answer the questions below.**

What is 20 feet (6.06 meters) long, 8 feet (2.44 meters) wide and 8.5 feet (2.59 meters) high? The answer is something which changed the world. This is the story of …

CONTAINERS

Cargo has travelled by sea for thousands of years. But in 1955, something happened which changed sea and other transport for ever: Malcolm McLean invented the container.
Mr McLean had a small trucking company in the USA. His idea was to use just one size of box for goods on his trucks and on ships. The boxes were 20 feet long, 8 feet wide and 8.5 feet high and this is still the normal size of a container.

Today, almost all transport of cargo is with containers. Why is a simple box so important? The first reason is that a container can travel by road, by train or by ship and the goods stay in the container. Before containers, people had to load and unload the goods all the time. The second important reason is that it's easy to load and unload containers at a port. Before containers it often took days or sometimes weeks to put hundreds of different things onto (and then to take them off) a ship. Today, in a big port like Hamburg, cranes can unload a big ship in only 4–5 hours. The third reason is that the goods in containers are safe. They don't break or get wet, and also people can't steal them – this was often a problem before containers.

Answer the questions in full sentences.

1 When did containers first begin?

____

2 How big is a container?

____

3 In what three different ways can a container travel?

____

4 How long does it take to unload a big ship today in a big port like Hamburg?

____

5 What was often a problem before container transport?

____

Unit 13 Global business

1 **Look at the pictures below and read how a typical supermarket company in the UK works.**

How a supermarket in the UK gets and sells its goods

1 First, the supermarket company's 'buyers' buy the goods. They buy some goods in the UK, but they buy a lot of things – like wine, and oranges and other fruit – in countries around the world.

2 Next, the supermarket company stores the goods. It stores them in big warehouses called 'distribution centres'. The company has distribution centres around the UK.

3 After that lorries transport the goods from the distribution centres to the different supermarkets. The lorries often deliver the goods at night, so that they are on sale fresh in the morning.

4 Finally, customers buy the goods at the supermarkets. At the checkouts, the checkout assistants put the barcodes of the goods into a computer. The company uses this information to order more goods.

2 **Now complete this text about the process. Use the *simple present passive*.**

First, the goods **(1)** __are bought__ **(buy)** by the company's buyers. Some goods **(2)** ____________ **(buy)** in the UK, but other goods **(3)** ____________ **(buy)** in countries around the world. Next the goods **(4)** ____________ **(store)** in big warehouses called distribution centres. After that the goods **(5)** ____________ **(transport)** by lorries to the company's supermarkets. The goods **(6)** ________ often ____________ **(deliver)** at night. Finally, the goods **(7)** ____________ **(buy)** by customers. The barcodes **(8)** ____________ **(put)** into a computer by the checkout assistants. This information **(9)** ____________ **(use)** by the supermarket to order more goods.

► **distribution centre** Vertriebszentrum ► **checkout** Kasse
► **checkout assistant** Kassierer/in ► **barcode** Strichcode

3 **What do you know about the history of these products from around the world? Try the quiz.**

1 popcorn	**2** aspirins	**3** paper	**4** chocolate

Everyone likes popcorn at the cinema. But who invented it? **a** Alfred T. Popcorn **b** Native Americans **c** Walt Disney	People use aspirins every day. But who invented them? **a** a German scientist **b** Mary-Ann Aspirin **c** an English scientist	Paper is 5,000 years old. But where was the first paper made? **a** in India **b** in France **c** in Egypt	When and where was chocolate discovered? **a** in 1500 in Europe **b** about 2,000 years ago in Mexico **c** 4,000 years ago in China
I think that popcorn was invented by ______ ______ ______	I think that aspirins were ______ ______ ______	I think that the first paper ______ ______ ______	Chocolate ______ ______ ______ ______

4 **Colour in the world map and write in the names of the places.**

Africa | Australia | Canada | China | Europe | India | Japan | USA
Mexico | New Zealand | Russia | Saudi Arabia | South America | Taiwan

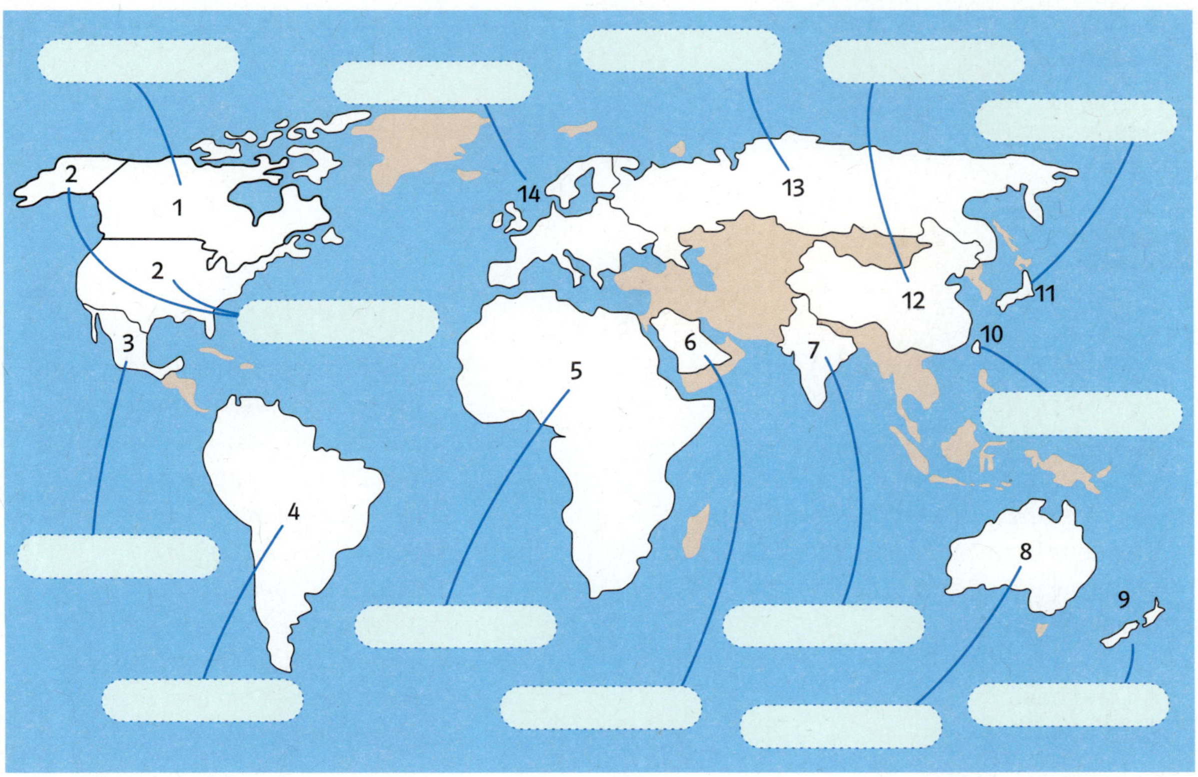

Emails at work

Hier lerne ich ...

→ einfache E-Mails auf Englisch richtig zu adressieren und formulieren.

5 **Sam Khan is an office assistant in a big international insurance company in London called Axxon. Sam is writing some emails this morning to colleagues in his company's offices around the world. He is asking his colleagues for different things. Look at the emails and answer the questions.**

1 Who are the emails to? What countries do they live in?

A: ______

B: ______

C: ______

2 In which email (A, B or C) does Sam ask for:

a an address? ______

b some dates? ______

c some telephone numbers ______

Email A

Postausgang

To:	Pete.Bradley@Axxon.au
Cc:	
Subject:	New extension numbers

Dear Pete
Hope all's well with you. Could you please send me a list of the new telephone extension numbers in the Sydney office? Many thanks in advance.

Best wishes
Sam

Email B

Postausgang

To:	Caterina.Pausini@Axxon.it
Cc:	
Subject:	Name of hotel in Rome?

Hello Caterina
How are you? Could you please let me have the name of the hotel in Rome where Mr Richardson stayed last month? He would like to use the hotel again next month.

Kind regards
Sam

Email C

Postausgang

To:	Heiko.Rausch@Axxon.at
Cc:	
Subject:	Dates of Mr Seifert's visit

Heiko, hope you're well. Could you please tell me the dates of Mr Seifert's visit to the London office next month? Thanks!

All the best
Sam

Hier und dort

In englischsprachigen Ländern sind E-Mails oft etwas informeller als im deutschen Geschäftsleben. Unter Arbeitskollegen sind Vornamen üblich, obwohl der Stil immer höflich bleibt. Mögliche Anreden für E-Mails sind: *Dear ..., Hello ...* oder nur der Name. Am Ende schreibt man gewöhnlich *Best wishes, Kind regards* oder *All the best* (manchmal *ATB* geschrieben).

6 **It's the next morning. Sam has the replies below to his emails.**

- Who wrote which email? Write in the names at the end of each email.
- Look at all the emails on this page and on the last page and complete the email phrases in the box.

Email 1

Posteingang

I'm fine thanks, Sam. And you?
Mr Seiffert will be in London from 16–21 May.

Best wishes

____

Email 2

Posteingang

Dear Sam

Things are hectic (as usual!). I'm attaching the extension numbers which you asked for. Let me know if you need anything else.

Kind regards

____

Email 3

Posteingang

Hello Sam

I'm very well thanks. Hope you are too. Here's the address of the hotel in Rome which you wanted:
Hotel Albani, Via dei Serpenti 109,
00184 Rome

ATB

____

Tips and tricks

So sagt man E-Mail-Adressen auf Englisch:

.	*dot*	-	*dash*
_	*underscore*	@	*at*

jean.carter@eurotech.com
= jean *dot* carter *at* eurotech *dot* com

Paul_Lanning@software.co.uk
= Paul *underscore* Lanning *at* software *dot* co *dot* uk

Email phrases

» Beginning an email
Dear … / Hello …
Hope all's **(1)** … with you.
How are you?
(2) … you're well.

» Asking for things
(3) … you please send me …?
Could you please **(4)** … me have …?
Could you please tell me …?

» Finishing an email
(Many) thanks in **(5)** … Thanks!
Best wishes
Kind **(6)** …
All **(7)** …

» Replying to an email
I'm fine / very well thanks.
And you? Hope you are too.
I'm **(8)** … the … which you asked for.
Here's … which you wanted.
Let me **(9)** … if you need anything else.

1 __________ **4** __________ **7** __________
2 __________ **5** __________ **8** __________
3 __________ **6** __________ **9** __________

7 **Now YOU. Work with a partner to write and reply to emails.**

- Write an email on another piece of paper to your partner. Ask for something in your email.
- Exchange emails with your partner and write a reply.
- Use the phrases from the last page. Think of addresses etc. yourself.
- Copy your two emails into Email 1 and 2 below.

Email 1

Postausgang

To:	
Cc:	
Subject:	

Email 2

Postausgang

To:	
Cc:	
Subject:	

Things you can write about:

1 You would like to know someone's email address / telephone number / mobile number.
2 A good hotel in Chicago?
3 A PDF of a brochure for a new product
4 The date(s) of a person's visit / a trade fair / a meeting
5 A copy of a report or an email
...

Unit 14 Job satisfaction

1 **Ben Cohen and Jerry Greenfield invented a famous product – yes, Ben & Jerry's ice cream. Read the notes about them then finish the sentences below. Use the *simple past* and the *past perfect*.**

Ben & Jerry's timeline

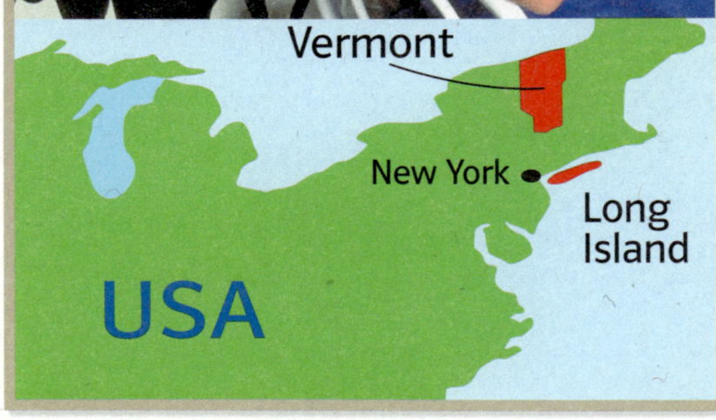

1973 Ben Cohen met Jerry Greenfield at high school on Long Island, New York. They became friends.

1977 The two friends finished high school then moved to a town in Vermont.

1978 They did a short course in how to make ice cream at a college. Then they opened an ice cream shop in their town. The shop was in an old gas station

1985 Lots of people bought the ice cream! Ben and Jerry opened an ice cream factory (also in Vermont).

1987 They sold their ice cream all around the USA.

1988 They opened a shop in Canada.

1994 They opened their first shop in England.

1996 They also started selling ice cream in other European countries.

1998 They opened shops in France and Japan.

2002 They opened their first shop in Germany.

1 After Ben ___had met___ **(meet)** Jerry at school, the two guys ___became___ **(become)** good friends.

2 After they ________ **(finish)** high school, they ________ **(move)** to a town in Vermont.

3 After they ________ **(do)** a short course about ice cream, they ________ **(open)** an ice cream shop in an old gas station in their town.

4 After lots of people ________ their ice cream, Ben and Jerry ________ a factory (also in Vermont).

5 After they ________ their ice cream all around the USA, they ________ a shop in Canada.

6 After they ________ ice cream shops in England, other European countries, France and Japan, they ________________

____

► **timeline** Zeitachse ► **gas station (US)** Tankstelle

2 **Read about Ben & Jerry's pizza, then finish the sentences. They are all if-*sentences type 3*.**

1 If Ben's name had been (be) Pete (not Ben), the name of the company ______ **(be)** Pete & Jerry's Ice Cream.

2 If Ben and Jerry hadn't been **(not/be)** at high school together, they ______ **(not/become)** friends.

3 And if they ______ **(not/become)** friends, they ______ **(not/start)** a company.

4 Everybody in their town liked Ben and Jerry's ice cream. But if people ______ **(hate)** it, then Ben and Jerry ______ **(close)** their shop. And today we wouldn't have Ben & Jerry's Ice Cream.

Hier und dort

Did you know?

Ben and Jerry's *first* idea wasn't to have an ice cream shop. They wanted to sell pizzas. If they had sold pizzas (and not ice cream), their company would have been *Ben & Jerry's Pizza*.

3 **Jerry Greenfield once said: "If work isn't fun, why do it?" Look back at this unit. What ideas about work can you find? What are your ideas – why do you want to have a job one day? What do you hope about your job? That it will be interesting? That you'll meets lots of people? Write about 100 words. Count the words at the end.**

Final test

Listening: The IceHotel

Hier überprüfe ich, was ich gelernt habe …

→ Hörverstehen
→ Leseverstehen
→ Sprachmittlung
→ Schreiben

2|15 **Listen to the radio interview. Which is right? Put √ in the box.**

1 The hotel Lisa works at is unusual because
☐ **a** it's in the north of Sweden.
☐ **b** it's made of ice.
☐ **c** it's only open from April to December.

2 The people who work at the IceHotel
☐ **a** need to work in minus temperatures.
☐ **b** don't have to wear warm clothes.
☐ **c** all live in igloos.

3 The guests have to bring
☐ **a** their own snow suits.
☐ **b** their own hats.
☐ **c** their own toothbrushes.

4 The rooms
☐ **a** have different prices.
☐ **b** are all one price.
☐ **c** are all the same size.

5 14,000 guests stayed in the IceHotel
☐ **a** this year.
☐ **b** in 1990.
☐ **c** last year.

6 The IceHotel in Sweden
☐ **a** was the first hotel made of ice.
☐ **b** is the biggest hotel made of ice.
☐ **c** is the coldest hotel made of ice.

7 The idea for the IceHotel started in an igloo. How?
☐ **a** Some ice artists showed their works there.
☐ **b** Some ice artists slept there.
☐ **c** Some visitors spent the night there.

Reading: **My own business**

Read about the small businesses and answer the questions.

Sue Ryan, personal shopper

I started working in a boutique on Saturdays when I was still at school and I often wished I had time to give people more help with the things they bought. So later I trained to be a personal shopper. At first I worked for a big department store. Now I work for myself and I do lots of different things. For example, I buy food for old people who can't leave their homes, I buy Christmas gifts for busy people, or business gifts for companies. I like my job and the best thing about it is that I can spend other people's money!

Tim Bennett, house and pet sitter

Everyone has heard of a baby sitter, but not many people have heard of a house and pet sitter. I look after people's houses, pets and plants while they are away. I put some adverts in the local paper to find my first customers. Now I have so many regular customers, I will soon need a partner to help me. The most interesting thing about this job is that everyone's house or pet or plants are different. It's important for me to find out the best way to look after them. After all, nobody wants to come back from their holidays to find that their favourite plant has died or their pet is ill.

Mike Lewis, driver

My small company offers a personal driver service. I started alone five years ago and now I have four other drivers who work for me. What does a personal driver do? Well, some people who have cars are not able or not allowed to drive. But they want to keep and use their cars. So they call us and we drive them to where they want to go. Sometimes it's to a personal appointment or on a shopping trip. Or perhaps they want us to take them to the airport or pick them up. Or they want to take a drive out in the country just for fun. These are just some of the things our clients want. Our slogan is "Just ask – we can do it!"

(360 words)

A True, false or not in the text?

	true	false	not in the text
1 Sue worked for a big department store.	☐	☐	☐
2 Companies spend a lot of money on Christmas gifts.	☐	☐	☐
3 Tim has a partner to help him.	☐	☐	☐
4 Tim went on a course to learn about plants and animals.	☐	☐	☐
5 Tim has more than enough work.	☐	☐	☐
6 There are five people in Mike's company.	☐	☐	☐
7 Mike only drives people who don't know how to drive.	☐	☐	☐
8 Some of Mike's customers have big, expensive cars.	☐	☐	☐

B Who asked the question? Write S (Sue), T (Tim) or M (Mike).

☐ Where would you like to go, Madam?

☐ Would you like some fresh milk, too?

☐ What time does your flight arrive?

☐ Does Bonzo have his meal in the morning or in the evening?

► **slogan** Werbespruch

Mediation: **Letter from England**

1 **Dein Chef hat diese E-Mail erhalten. Er spricht leider kein Englisch. Erkläre ihm sinngemäß auf Deutsch, was die E-Mail beinhaltet.**

Dear Mr Berendt,

I am writing to say that I will be in Cologne in September. We have only corresponded by email so far, and I would very much like to meet you personally while I am in Germany.

I plan to be in Cologne from 17–21 September. Could you let me know what would be a good time for you for a meeting? I have meetings all day on the 19th, but would be free on the other days. Also, where would you like to meet? I could come to your office, or we could meet at my hotel.

Looking forward to hearing from you soon.

2 **Ein junger Engländer macht ein Praktikum in Ihrem Büro. Sein Deutsch ist noch nicht sehr gut. Er interessiert sich für einen Artikel über Einkaufen im Internet, kann ihn aber leider nicht so gut verstehen. Erkläre ihm sinngemäß auf Englisch, worum es geht.**

Machen Sie Ihren wöchentlichen Supermarkteinkauf doch einfach im Internet. Sie finden eine große Auswahl an Lebensmitteln und anderen Supermarkt-Artikeln, welche Sie bequem und einfach über das Internet bestellen und Ihre Bestellung wird zu Ihnen nach Hause gebracht.

Zwischen der Bestellung im Internet und der Lieferung liegen meistens 1-2 Tage. Der Einkauf über den Lebensmittel Shop im Internet eignet sich dadurch auch hervorragend um größere Mengen, z. B. für eine Party, schnell und problemlos einzukaufen.

Besonders geeignet ist der **Supermarkt im Internet** für Personen die aufgrund von z. B. Krankheiten das Haus nicht verlassen können, oder kein Auto haben.

Online Supermark

Writing: **Booking a room**

Your boss is going to London and she has asked you to book a single room for her in the City Hotel, 3 Tooting St., London SW1H 9LA. Write to the hotel.

Don't forget:
- your boss's full name
- the room must have a shower
- the number of nights and the dates

Ask about:
- the price of a room per night
- breakfast in the price?
- English breakfast?
- how to get there from the airport

Vocabulary

Unbekannte Wörter wurden nur einmal aufgenommen; in späteren Units werden sie als bekannt vorausgesetzt. Wörter, die in den Fußnoten der Language-practice-Seiten übersetzt sind, wurden nicht aufgenommen.

Schreibe deinen eigenen Satz.

Unit 1 An application form

application form	Bewerbungsformular	
capital letter	Großbuchstabe	
date of birth	Geburtsdatum	
first name	Vorname	
nationality	Staatsangehörigkeit	
post code	Postleitzahl	
surname	Nachname	

Unit 2 In the office

calendar	Kalender	
computer screen	Computerbildschirm	
diary	Terminkalender	
filing cabinet	Aktenschrank	
keyboard	Tastatur	
plant	Pflanze	
radiator	Heizkörper	
shelf	Regal	
waste bin	Abfalleimer	

Unit 3 A company website

award	Auszeichnung	
basket	Korb	
button	Knopf	

		Schreibe deinen eigenen Satz.
careers	*hier:* Stellenangebote	
contact	Kontakt	
customer	Kunde/Kundin	
equipment	Ausstattung	
furniture	Möbel	
news	Neuigkeiten	
to sell something online	etwas online verkaufen	
store	Geschäft	

Unit 4 Departments in a company

to advertise	für etwas werben	
customer service	Kundendienst	
distribution	Vertrieb	
finance	Finanz-	
marketing	Marketing	
production	Produktion	
research and development	Forschung und Entwicklung	
sales	Verkauf	

Unit 5 Clothes for work

blouse	Bluse	
dark	dunkel-	
jacket	Jacke, Sakko	
shirt	Hemd	
skirt	Rock	
spotted	gepunktet	
striped	gestreift	
suit	Anzug	

		Schreibe deinen eigenen Satz.

Unit 6 On the phone (1)

Could I speak to ..., please?	Könnte ich bitte mit ... sprechen?	
Hold the line, please.	Bleiben Sie am Apparat, bitte.	
I'll put you through.	Ich stelle Sie durch.	
Ltd (Limited)	Gesellschaft mit beschränkter Haftung	
to spell	buchstabieren	
Who's calling, please?	Wer ist am Apparat, bitte?	

Unit 7 On the phone (2)

Can he call you back?	Kann er Sie zurückrufen?	
Can I take your number?	Dürfte ich Ihre Nummer notieren?	
How can I help you?	Wie kann ich Ihnen helfen?	
I'm sorry, ... isn't here at the moment	Es tut mir leid, ... ist momentan nicht da.	

Unit 8 At the reception desk

appointment	Termin	
arrival	Ankunft	
at all times	die ganze Zeit	
signature	Unterschrift	
to take a seat	Platz nehmen, sich setzen	
visitor's badge	Besucherausweis	
visitor's book	Besucherbuch	

Schreibe deinen eigenen Satz.

Unit 9 Booking a hotel room

bill	Rechnung
to confirm a booking	eine Buchung bestätigen
to do something straight away	etwas sofort tun
to make a booking	buchen
to make arrangements	Vorbereitungen treffen

Unit 10 An enquiry

advertisement	Werbung, Anzeige
to be grateful (for)	dankbar sein (für)
current	aktuell
Dear Sir or Madam.	Sehr geehrte Damen und Herren,
delivery times	Lieferzeiten
in advance	im Voraus
manufacturing	Produktion
purchasing manager	Einkaufsleiter/in
recent	unlängst, kürzlich
trade discount	Handelsrabatt
trade fair	Handelsmesse
trade journal	Fachzeitschrift
Yours faithfully,	Mit freundlichen Grüßen (wenn der Empfänger mit *Dear Sir or Madam* angesprochen wird)
Yours sincerely,	Mit freundlichen Grüßen (wenn der Empfänger persönlich angesprochen wird)

		Schreibe deinen eigenen Satz.

Unit 11 An offer

discount	Rabatt	
on display	ausgestellt	
to expect	erwarten	
to hesitate	zögern	
immediately	sofort	
impressed	beeindruckt	
to include	beinhalten, einschließen	
insurance	Versicherung	
offer	Angebot	
payment (in full)	Bezahlung (gesamt)	
port	Hafen	
quotation	Kostenvoranschlag	
to receive	erhalten	
reply	Antwort	
shortly	in Kürze	
terms of payment	Zahlungsbedingungen	
trade	Handel	
transport	Fracht	

Unit 12 An order

consignment	Warensendung	
crane	Kran	
further	weitere	
item	Artikel	
on receipt of	nach Erhalt von	
to place an order	eine Bestellung aufgeben	

		Schreibe deinen eigenen Satz.
satisfied	zufrieden	
to steal (stole, stolen)	stehlen	
trial order	Probeauftrag	
trucking company *(US)*	Speditionsfirma	
wide	breit	

Unit 13 Emails at work

All the best	Alles Gute	
to attach	anhängen	
Best wishes	Mit besten Grüßen	
extension number	Durchwahlnummer	
Kind regards	Mit freundlichen Grüßen	
office assistant	Büroassistent/in	

COV: Avenue Images GmbH (Image Source RF), Hamburg, Fotosearch RF (Getty RF), Waukesha, WI; S. 4 1: iStockphoto (Julie Deshaies), Calgary, Alberta; S. 4 2: Fotosearch RF (Design Pics), Waukesha, WI; S. 5 1: Ernst Klett Sprachen GmbH, Stuttgart; S. 7 1: Dreamstime (John Casey), Brentwood, TN, 2: Dreamstime (Sebastian Czapnik), Brentwood, TN, 3: shutterstock (Gina Smith), New York, NY, 4: shutterstock (Raisa Kanareva), New York, NY, 5: Dreamstime (Zachary Pelka), Brentwood, TN, 6: iStockphoto (Chris Schmidt), Calgary, Alberta, 7: iStockphoto (Bojan Tezak), Calgary, Alberta; S. 8 1: shutterstock (Bartosz Ostrowski), New York, NY, 2: iStockphoto (Lise Gagne), Calgary, Alberta, 3: iStockphoto (Alexey Stiop), Calgary, Alberta, 4: iStockphoto (Helen Rubtsov), Calgary, Alberta, 5: iStockphoto (Franziska Richter), Calgary, Alberta, 6: shutterstock (EuToch), New York, NY, A008.8: iStockphoto (Eliza Snow), Calgary, Alberta; S. 11 1: iStockphoto (Chris Schmidt), Calgary, Alberta, 2: JupiterImages (photos.com), Tucson, AZ; S. 12 1: shutterstock (Dima Potemkin), New York, NY, 2: iStockphoto, Calgary, Alberta; S. 13 1: iStockphoto (Andrea Gingerich), Calgary, Alberta, 2: JupiterImages (photos.com), Tucson, AZ, 3: shutterstock (Jyothi Joshi), New York, NY, 4: iStockphoto (Lance Bellers), Calgary, Alberta, 5: iStockphoto (Matthew Scherf), Calgary, Alberta, 6: iStockphoto (David Lewis), Calgary, Alberta; S. 14 1: Corbis (Atlantide Phototravel), Düsseldorf; S. 15 1: Action Press (Hans-Georg Gaul), Hamburg, 2: Bananastock RF, Watlington / Oxon, 3: shutterstock (Laurence Gough), New York, NY, 4: iStockphoto (Alex Gumerov), Calgary, Alberta, 5: iStockphoto (Abimelec Olan), Calgary, Alberta, 6: iStockphoto (Radu Razvan), Calgary, Alberta, 7: iStockphoto (Millanovic), Calgary, Alberta; S. 16 1: BigStockPhoto.com (philw), Davis, CA, 2: BigStockPhoto.com (pattie), Davis, CA; S. 17 1: JupiterImages (photos.com), Tucson, AZ, 2: Alfred Kärcher Vertriebs-GmbH, Winnenden, 3: Alfred Kärcher Vertriebs-GmbH, Winnenden; S. 18 1: iStockphoto (Andrew Howe), Calgary, Alberta, 2: Dreamstime (Eastwest Imaging), Brentwood, TN, 3: iStockphoto (Ana Abejon), Calgary, Alberta; S. 19 1: JupiterImages (photos.com), Tucson, AZ, 2: JupiterImages (photos.com), Tucson, AZ, 3: JupiterImages (photos.com), Tucson, AZ, 4: shutterstock (Kovalev Serguei), New York, NY, 5: Dreamstime (Iurii Lupol), Brentwood, TN, 6: JupiterImages (photos.com), Tucson, AZ; S. 20 Internet / Screenshot (www.pateno1.de); S. 21 Dreamstime (Dreamstime.com Agency), Brentwood, TN; S. 22 Dreamstime (Tomasz Trojanowski), Brentwood, TN; S. 23 1: iStockphoto (Cora Reed), Calgary, Alberta, 2: Comstock (Comstock (Luxemburg)), Luxemburg, 3: Comstock (Comstock (Luxemburg)), Luxemburg; S. 24 Dreamstime (Dreamstime.com Agency), Brentwood, TN; S. 26 1: BigStockPhoto.com (sonyae), Davis, CA, 2: iStockphoto (ooyoo), Calgary, Alberta, 3: iStockphoto (Windzepher), Calgary, Alberta; S. 27 iStockphoto (Trista Weibell), Calgary, Alberta; S. 28 1: Airbus Deutschland GmbH (Airbus S.A.S. Computer Modeling & Render), Hamburg, 2, 3, 4: Flughafen Köln / Bonn, Köln; S. 30 BigStockPhoto.com (Yuri_Arcurs), Davis, CA; S. 31 1: shutterstock (Margaret Smeaton), New York, NY, 2: iStockphoto (Steve Geer), Calgary, Alberta, : BigStockPhoto.com (khz), Davis, CA, 4: shutterstock (Leah-Anne Thompson), New York, NY; S. 34 1: iStockphoto (Achim Prill), Calgary, Alberta, 2: iStockphoto (Justin Horrocks), Calgary, Alberta; S. 35 1: Messe Berlin GmbH, Berlin, 2: PhotoDisc; S. 40 iStockphoto (Ivan Mateev), Calgary, Alberta; S. 43 1: Dreamstime (Hannamariah), Brentwood, TN, 2: shutterstock (Timothy Large), New York, NY, 3: Alamy Images RM (JL Photography), Abingdon, Oxon, 4: Alamy Images RM (Worldwide Picture Library), Abingdon, Oxon; S. 45 1: iStockphoto (Olga Shelego), Calgary, Alberta, 2: iStockphoto (Don Bayley), Calgary, Alberta; S. 47 1: iStockphoto (Dan Barnes), Calgary, Alberta, 2: iStockphoto (Joerg Reimann), Calgary, Alberta; S. 48 1: Corbis (GIRAUD PHILIPPE), Düsseldorf, 2: shutterstock (JoLin), New York, NY, 3: Internet / Screenshot (Len Roger's Collecti), 4: Avenue Images GmbH (Corbis RF), Hamburg; S. 49 1: Creativ Collection Verlag GmbH, Freiburg, 2: iStockphoto (Angelo Marcantonio), Calgary, Alberta, 4: iStockphoto (RF / Jon Helgason), Calgary, Alberta; W050.1: iStockphoto (ronen), Calgary, Alberta; S. 53 Corbis (Richard T. Nowitz), Düsseldorf; S. 55 shutterstock (Helmut Konrad Watson), New York, NY; S. 56 1: BigStockPhoto.com (Dmitry Romanchuck), Davis, CA, 2: BigStockPhoto.com (Pavel Losevsky), Davis, CA, 3: iStockphoto (Gary Martin), Calgary, Alberta.